"Don't Let the Prett

EMBEDDED SEEDS

My story proves that destructive behavior CAN be laid to rest; the sun CAN shine and a broken soul CAN be repaired once you understand the truth.

"Change is possible once you realize it's <u>your</u> choice."

**"In the beginning God created light
and dark, and it was good."**
Genesis

If I had only known that both good and evil would be a part of my life, maybe I would have done better. My goal with this book is to keep it real and represent the actual events as they took place. That includes occasional language and vivid imagery.

So, in the forthcoming chapters, I use the language that was applicable for that time so please bear that in mind. After all, "There's a time and place for everything."

"Everything has a season."
Proverbs

My goal...

To reach out to the future generations; particularly the at-risk individuals that are living, have lived or headed towards destructive lifestyles.

I will provide knowledge through self-experiences that change is possible once you realize that positive change is your choice.

I will give this knowledge by way of allowing the doors of my life to open for individuals to read and visualize the path I took to get where I am today.

The following sequels of "***Don't Let the Pretty Face Fool Ya***" will lay bare the interactions with family friends and events that I experienced and survived. I will describe the mental and physical affects that I experienced before, during, and after the encounters with those individuals and events.

I will provide a way for others to understand and learn from my journey how they too can survive and change a destructive life into a positive one.

Don't Let the Pretty Face Fool Ya!
Embedded Seeds

Tonie Punch Author
Indianapolis, Indiana (Born)
Houston, Texas

Raw content, No edit
Mentorial Hayes book cover design & interior photos
Gerald Wright, Recent photos of Tonie Punch

Anthony Stillwell/PR & Marketing

Antoinette "Tonie" Punch Founder/Youth & Community
Advocate/Speaker/Writer

For Inquiries and Booking Information

Please Contact:
http://www.ToniePunch.com
info@toniepunch.com
1-888-289-1088

ISBN-13: 978-1466224063
ISBN-10: 1466224061

Printed in the United Stated of America

DEDICATIONS

Samuel, Byron, Jeremy, Syamon, Baby Tonie (September 23, 1991, stillbirth) and Victor, without the love for you all to keep me strong I would not have made it through my destructive lifestyle. The smiles, hugs, and the shared words "I love you Momma", gave me the determination to make a change.

Not just for you but for myself. It has been my pleasure to watch each one of you grow and I thank you for sharing that with me. Thank you for your patience as I continue to work hard to be your mother.

Knowing that one-day you would have to face the world, and all of its possessions, was the most influential factor in sharing my story. I felt it is necessary in order to give you an understanding of generational cycles and the tools to reclaim yourself. For you to know what I went through that made me the person I was and how I broke my generational cycle to be the person I am today.

My ultimate hope is that you will not only use my knowledge in your own life but in your parenting lives in the future.

Don't allow my negative past to consume your thoughts. Please understand you don't have to live life from the patterns I laid before you. You have the control to make positive decisions for your own lives and what you choose to instill in your own children as they grow and watch you.

Thank you.

Regardless of my neglects as a mother, you all have stood beside me and loved me unconditionally for being your mother. Likewise, the love I hold for all of you grows daily and will never be consumed- it is a seed that will grow forever.

Never let go, never stop fighting and always be accountable for your choices.

To my grandchildren, I am so proud to have each one of you.

To my husband Greg, thank you.

You gave me everything I needed to face my past and move forward to a brighter future. You didn't judge me or condemn me for my negative ways, nor turn from me because of my flaws. You accepted a ready-made family, and you hung in here with us through it all. For this, I want you to know how truly thankful I am to have you and how beautiful my life has become with your unconditional love for me.

READER COMMENTS

"But Jesus called the children to him and said, *"Let the little children come to me, and do not hinder them, for the kingdom of God belongs to such as these."* Luke 18:16. That scripture seems as far from the reality of Tonie Punch's childhood as the East is from the West... as the Kingdom of Heaven is from the very pit of hell. *"Don't Let the Pretty Face Fool Ya! Embedded Seeds: The Beginning"*, a book that describes (but hardly explains) the life and suffering of the author, Tonie Punch, literally proves beyond a shadow of a doubt that Satan comes only to *steal* and *kill* and *destroy*.

But, it also proves that the Love of God can reach beyond any circumstances, no matter how far we may fall and no matter how lost we may believe we are. As long as His grace abounds, even when we make our bed in hell, He is always with us.

With God, we are never out of sight or never out of mind.

I have met Tonie Punch face-to-face, and we have spoken woman-to-woman. But, after reading *Embedded Seeds*, I have not been able to shake the little girl, Tonie, the little girl crying out to be saved. We are each accountable for her in some way. She has been robbed of her innocence, taught to hate who she was born to be, and nearly destroyed by a force of evil that she was much too young and fragile to reckon with.

This demonic spirit hid itself like a thief and a coward within the life of Tonie's mother; the one person that should have loved and protected her chose to become Tonie's greatest enemy.

Embedded Seeds is a true story of "raw and real" pain, which by the grace of God, Tonie Punch lives today to write and speak about. If this book offends or makes the reader angry --it should. I pray this book is an offense to everyone that reads it, and makes us all angry enough to reach out and save a child from the bad choices of his/her parents and from the hands of an abuser.

The life of Tonie Punch did not evolve. Her life was created, and her creator is accountable for all that she suffered.

--Donna L. Patton,
Founder/President, WeAreFearless.com
Author, *From Faythe to Ever-Increasing Faith*
Contributing author, *100 Words of Wisdom for Women*

Embedded Seeds is a story from the heart of a woman who is brave enough to confront her past no matter how ugly it can be. Physical beauty can be a curse when the ugliness of violence, ignorance, and sexual impropriety are part of one's daily experience of growing up. I get the feeling when reading Tonie's story that she is well on her way to breaking the cycle into which she was born.

Her story is really a universal one that can show us all something about who we are and how to look at where we come from and where we are going.

Lee Ajamu Means, J.D.

"Don't Let The Pretty Face Fool Ya",

Consumed my Soul, this book opens the door of discovery for those who have had painful childhoods' that ultimately led to choosing addictive behavior patterns.

Encompassed in this book are challenges to look within and focus on God given Gifts while tapping into the forgotten dreams of the inner-child.

It gives us permission to realize that pain is necessary in order for us to step into our True-Self. I have been pivoted to continue my journey through Recovery with renewed dignity. Tonie's writing is confirmation that we all have a Purpose in this thing called Life!

Continued Peace & Prosperity Tonie Punch!

Sheila Rivers
Grateful Recovering Addict

INSPIRATIONS

Vida Carter

Vida, you hold a place in my heart and I will love you for life. Over the years we have built a strong bond for one another; first my client, then my friend, my sister in Christ, and a respected woman that I want and need in my life. Thank you for your honesty, debates, and support in moving me towards my life's calling. You are a blessing to me and no words can express how thankful I am to have you on my side.

Debra Means

Debra, you have been the mother-figure I never had. Thank you! Starting as my client and over time inspiring (from the love in your heart) me to open up my mouth and mind to what God has in store for my life. You wouldn't give up or allow me to stop seeking my dreams. Your unconditional love relieves me, heals, and pushes me forward. Thank you from the depths of my heart.

Kamia Jackson

Kamia, my sister you are so dear to me. The love we share is like no other. You walked into my life a stranger and made your place untouchable. You are there for me in more ways than a few. Your love and support has helped me grow. You give of yourself so freely, providing me with guidance and filling a spot in my life that is unexplainable.

You and your family took us in and we share not only motherhood but sisterhood. Thank you sis for all you are and all you provide to my spirit.

Nate Rush

Nate, Nate, Nate…thank you. You know my passion personally. You opened up a part of my mind and serve as my own personal first-aid kit for many of my hurts. You gave me the time, guidance and strength to cross many stumps in my path. You believe in me and my vision.

Nate, you are an important person in my life and you encourage me to go after my goals. Again thank you.

Gerald Wright

Gerald, our time together hasn't been long but it has been so fulfilling. One meeting was all it took. You recognized my passion to help the community and without hesitation, you opened my first door here in Indy. You not only heard my words but you felt my drive and you provide a tool for me to unleash. Thank you for being who you are and believing in me.

Mack Bone

Mack, you walked in my door and right off the back we made a connection. We share a passion for our visions, dreams, hopes and goals. You are a male version of my life struggles and without shame we share our experiences and inspirations. Mack you told me how much I have inspired you; however you inspired me too. You walk a time line like no other but when I need your help you make your time mine. Mack all I can say is "Ditto". Keep it as real.

There are several more people I could mention and I pray they know who they are. Please know that each one of you have participated in molding the person I have become and I thank you all. Strangers before… family now! Thank you for your open minds and ears, your input, and belief in me.

ACCEPTANCE OF MY CHOICE

To my family; in the beginning, I was going to name names and place blame, but it isn't about that. This is about me and the life I had to live and the memories embedded in my mind. I am hoping that through sharing the life I lived, I can help at least one person.

The seeds I grew from to the product that came from those seeds, to this day, I'm not proud of, but okay with it.

I have no shame about the hell that I have experienced and witnessed in my life. I have no regrets either. I thank my Higher Power for yesterday, today and tomorrow. If I had not lived these experiences, I wouldn't be the woman I am today and the passion that grows in my heart wouldn't be alive.

To anyone that may be offended, I don't apologize. I do hope you find it in your heart to accept that, yes; this was a part of your past. So move on - I did!

I wrote these memories from my past for personal reasons. The ones I didn't write about may also surface one day. I owe no one an explanation for my choices because this book was and is my choice. My past was a cycle of my life I had to live to become who I am today. Today, I have a life.

To my friends; your support of my vision and passion has given me the strength to hang on when I did not see a reason to. Not one of you pushed me away because of my past.

Hell, I feel knowing and accepting me for who I was and am today made our relationships stronger. You accepted my family as well and have shown support and love for us, and for this, I personally thank each and every one of you.

For those that know me and didn't believe in me or had no positive direction to give me because of my past, thank you too. The strength I received from those that looked upon me as a *statistic* was just the inspiration I needed to accomplish my dreams.

Determination boiled in me due to all who made negative statements, or showed no support because of my past and my bad situations made you doubt my sincerity.

I want you to know, "My dreams and passion *are real*", so all I can say to you is, "Look at me now *"Don't Let the Pretty Face Fool Ya!"* Nothing, and definitely no one, can stop what is God driven! And to the rest-*"**Change is possible once you realize that change is <u>your choice</u>"!***

Naïve Mind

My memories would not be pleasant for most. They are full of lies, fears, confusion, and hopeless outcomes. Some memories were tragic, not only to the mind, but physically scarring to my heart. From my first black eye, to the door that split my scalp, growing up was one nightmare after another...watching actions of adults and teens a child my age should not have witnessed.

My mother and the females in my life should have taught me about the things a little girl should know and should have kept me away from the things that I do know now. I needed guidance and love from all those in my life and only received lessons of the hell their lives were traveling.

Take this walk down memory lane as I allow your mind to envision the seeds embedded in mine...These memories started at three years of age and the story goes like this...

Life was full of mind-boggling experiences and curious questions left unanswered. Those mind-boggling experiences started in a little two bedroom, one bath brick house with a red and a white porch and window covers.

At three, I was living a life of a 13 year old. I grew older and at a much faster pace in the mind than any little girl should have. *I can imagine the look on your face! However, it is true.*

I faced challenges that laid like alligators in the swamp for my unknowing mind and body; not to mention my undeveloped view of life.

After the birth of my baby brother in 1974, my young eyes began to see things that would leave damaging memories in every corner of my mind. With this knowledge, these memories would come to be the stones that I used to step on with every passing year of growth.

That first black eye came from jumping in the neighbor's bed and led to the first touch from a male between my thighs. That touch made me wonder what was my kitty-cat really used for; r*eality was telling me it wasn't just used to pee-pee.*

Watching as the fighting among my parents and family members happened before my eyes, I began to think of it as if watching TV; *there was no stopping it* and we never had a boring night. I even had to deal with the men that came in and out of my mother's door, so I made a game of it; balling up my fist and opening it one finger at a time, *my beginning stage of counting* as I watched each man that entered the house.

My first known father belonged to my baby brother. He would come and go with the wind. When he needed to be away from his wife, he would stay with my mother. He did show me love as a father but he also marked my inner spirit with the drama between a man and a woman. Do not get it twisted; momma played her role too…oh yes she did!

As you engage in this intimate personal conversation with me, the scenes and dialogues that I share in this book, I believe will allow you to be there with me or reminisce upon your own experiences.

My aim is to provide a looking glass, a "crystal ball", to guard against unnecessary despair, in hopes that by learning and knowing of my personal life experiences, "better", can be achieved. To identify my cycle I had to re-live these memories, allow myself to visualize my challenges and expose my experiences so that I could move toward aiding my self-created freedom for change.

This is only my beginning. Change doesn't come over night or without life issues, so in order to see my change you must walk the complete path I provide for you with the sequels to follow. Now let's rap about some of the issues I was dealing with and the craziness before my eyes.

Remember I was young and naïve and my unhealthy environment raised my maturity level quickly…

Stripped Of My Innocence

My stepbrother was the first male to touch me between my thighs. He was back and forth between his mother's house and ours.

The events I lived were not pleasant and sickening to think about then and now. However, during the ins and outs of my mother's relationship with my baby brother's father, I had to deal with this stepbrother.

He was the oldest of us all and with his eyes on me; my stepbrother had the advantage over not only me, but the other kids too. He was left in charge whenever our parents went out or were not at home.

This allowed him the ability to use his authority along with his sick thoughts to begin kissing and touching me in my private area.

The first time he made a move on me I was scared as hell and was not sure what he was doing or how I was to respond. He made me sit on his lap and played with me in a touchy kind of manner.

He made up silly games in order to keep his hands on me.

His activities toward me became constant and obvious to the point that the other two stepbrothers started paying attention.

Not realizing how obvious he was to the other kids, he was caught holding me down as he climbed on top of me in the bed by my other stepbrothers. For me, this added stress to the situation because now I had to fight off more than one stepbrother at the same time. *As sure as I am telling my story, the fight was on.*

He didn't hesitate getting them involved with trying to *oochie coochie* me in order to keep them from telling on him.

My stepbrother became a daily threat and because of his advances, he would butter me up every chance he could.

Like a skilled con-artist, he offered snacks or allowed me to go outside to make sure no one told about his sick secrets. He used this same method to keep me from telling that he whipped my baby brother and me when our parents left, as he constantly made promises that he would not touch me or hump on me any more…nor involve his brothers in messing with me.

You can imagine that all of his, "I'm sorry", grew as sick as he was.

As I tried to understand what my stepbrother was doing to me, it frustrated me to the point that my reaction to him was to run, cry and scream, "I'm going to tell", as I begged him to stop.

These experiences with him started my curiosity about what the adults around me were into. I'd sneak around paying attention to what they were doing…watching the adults, somewhat gave me an understanding of what my stepbrother was trying to do with me.

It did not stop with him or them during that time. He continued to make empty promises of not messing with me, but his promises were straight bull.

Things got worse being home alone with my stepbrothers.

It turned into dealing with them holding me down, as one would get on top of me, humping me while I cried over their laughter.

The oldest got comfortable with his authority and being able to get the other brothers involved; therefore, he got bold and felt it was time to take his game to another level.

One night standing in the hallway holding me around my waist, he ordered the other boys to pull down their pants.

They were standing in the doorway of the bedroom. They pulled their pants down and just as he folded over my back making me fall forward to the floor, we heard the voices of our parents.

The younger two grabbed for their pants in a hurry to get them up, as my older stepbrother changed the tone from trying to fondle me, to acting as if we were wrestling by the time the door opened. His change of the scene, gave a look of innocent behavior.

Lord only knew how bad I wanted to tell on my stepbrothers and how scared I was of them at the same time. After enduring this behavior from them over and over again, I developed a hatred for the oldest stepbrother, because he was the reason I was dealing with that inappropriate acts. I began to pray for him to go home and never come back.

Each time he was interrupted, I knew my ass was only saved for the moment.

I do not recall my stepbrother whipping his brothers because they really did not live with us; they were only there on a day or two bases each time they were with us. My stepbrother stopped whipping me only because of his sick behaviors with me, but he continued to whip my baby brother. He would even whip him with his diaper off at times *Yep a baby!*

I remember as clear as day when my stepbrother was exposed for one of his crimes. He had gotten pissed at me for playing and waking up the baby. Once the baby started to cry and he couldn't shut him up so he ripped off his diaper, turned him face down on the back of the couch and started popping him on the ass with his hand.

I was mad as hell and I began to curse at him.

My mouth instantly shut when the door slammed behind me. I was hollering so loud, I did not even hear my mother when she walked in, but she heard me! The words rolling off my tongue is all her ears heard, so I had no choice but to explain why.

With me facing trouble for my cursing, this was the first time I told on my stepbrother. Telling about him whipping my baby brother sparked words between our parents. After the argument was over my oldest stepbrother got in big trouble, he got his ass beat and was grounded.

My stepbrother constantly seemed to walk around with an attitude. I felt it had a lot to do with; #1…he had to live at our house, and #2…he always was left to baby-sit us.

If I could only find the courage to tell everything that he was doing, especially what he did to me…but I was so scared of what would happen. Most of my fear came from him brainwashing me into not telling our parents by assuring me that he would get in trouble, and I would too.

He would then say, "After our punishment, you know our parents will still leave me in charge", and he would make me pay for telling. I felt I was in a "no-win" situation.

My hatred grew and I began to express outwardly my hatred toward him by not talking to him or leaving the room when he entered. I made threatening comments to him around the house.

Those comments let him know I no longer cared about getting in trouble. I added I would tell daddy instead of momma…that struck a nerve in him, because he did back off, at least for the moment.

The boy was cold hearted because he found other ways of causing me misery. He switched over to making fun of my nationality and assuring me that his family did not accept us…*my baby brother and I.*

Back in the seventies, here in Indianapolis, from my knowledge and the conversations around me, interracial couples were not accepted. My older stepbrother took it upon himself to explain to me that I was a zebra.

He put me in front of the bathroom mirror as he made comments like "your momma wants black kids, but you are not black…you're a white and black zebra without the stripes." He'd hold my jaws tight in the palms of his hands, so tight that my face would hurt for a while after he let me go.

He tortured me daily reminding me of my mixed heritage as if it was something to be ashamed of. His brother followed suit, compounding the torture I endured.

Their torture came to a brief end. The arguing between our parents would put the space I so badly needed between our families and giving me a break from them.

However, a cousin from that side of the family picked up torturing me in a different way. This cousin that continued the torture was a teenager and working on a career as a *hot tail,* running the streets on the regular.

My cousin would play mother in the daytime to my brother and me, and hit the streets at night with my mother or the man of the week. Being under my mother's roof was freedom for my cousin, or at least that is what I saw it as. I am not sure of her age at that time but she was young.

I watched the activities she stayed twisted in. Her activities helped my undeveloped mind focus on experiences I already lived with my stepbrothers. This would eventually enhance the curious thoughts going through my head. *However, I really was not prepared for the world awaiting me, but I continued to watch and learn.*

My cousin was the first to give me a whipping from hell. In other words, she put her signature across my ass.

One afternoon I stood in the next-door neighbor's yard, looking into a huge hole dug the day before. I lost my balance, which caused me to fall face first to the bottom of what felt like a pit inside. I was stuck in that hole for a long time, hollering and crying for someone but mainly my cousin to come get me out. Looking up scared as hell, all I could think about was snakes coming through the dirt, being covered up with dirt, or buried.

One of the boys from the house on the other side of our house heard me hollering and came to see what I was doing in this hole. He bent over the hole with a smile on his face. He teased me before pulling me out.

This made me mad and my anger tickled him red. He found it funny to see me suffering and not able to get myself out of the hole I was stuck in. He eventually pulled me up.

Muddy from head to toe, I went in the house only to become even angrier. My cousin had no problem with making sure I knew who was in control. At the top of her lungs, she hollered for me to get out of my clothes and in the tub. While I got out of those filthy clothes, she ran water for my bath.

Not thinking about the consequences because I was pissed, I did not realize what was in store for me once I entered the bathroom.

Forewarned that she wanted to tear into my butt for the last few weeks, now she had her chance and she was ready to beat me colorful. And she did!

Out of my clothes, I headed to take that bath. When my toes touched the water the heat sizzled up my leg and she gave me no chance to move any other way but forward. The scorching hot water gave aid to the switch she used to beat my ass and the sting was unbearable. Damn, my legs, arms and back felt as if my skin tore with every lick.

Once that ass whipping was over, she did not need to threaten me anymore, I was a believer. When I calmed down, I told her I was not going to tell momma. I knew she would get me again if I did.

On the cool, she pretty much allowed me to rip and run as I pleased, so I just stayed out of her way as much as possible. Especially now that she had signed her name my ass. I knew that she was there only for the moment and would be gone soon, but only to return again…!

The boy who pulled me out of the hole was the next male to play between my legs. His family was like family to us and I played at their house all the time. There were four children to my recollection, two girls and two boys. The youngest daughter was my playmate, at least in the beginning.

The boy that helped me out of the hole started showing me attention as if to like me. *Why? I do not have a clue…I was much younger than him.* Receiving his attention I showed interest back and found myself, I suppose, liking him too.

Allowing him to talking me into going to the back bedroom and playing a game of either house or doctor. I know while reading this you're probably thinking, "What the hell were you doing playing games like that?" I can only say that I was around four and naïve.

But by this time, I was a little too advanced in my mind for a girl my age, and curious about what a man and woman did in the bedroom when the door was closed.

From my encounter with my stepbrothers, the conversations with my cousin and being nosey as hell, this kept me wanting to learn more. Yes, all this craziness in my head and eyesight ignited my boldness and I stopped the crying and running.

While I acted as the mommy, the boy next door played the daddy role…or doctor and nurse at times. I would play along until it was time to go to bed with *sunshine outside, it was nighttime inside.* We would put the baby dolls to sleep…*they were the kids*; it would be the parents' time to do the *oochie-coochie* and my time to freeze up, in other words get scared.

He was not in any hurry, he made me feel it was okay to be scared and telling me to lie beside him in the bed. He played the understanding about my hesitation; I was his bait to reel in. He took his time and was careful to make sure I did not get scared enough to tell.

On our first couple of attempts to go all the way, we would lie in the bed with our clothes on and he would get on top of me...softy and slowly humping me. However, I did not realize this was another ploy to hook and soon reel me in. Each time we played, I became more and more comfortable.

I got so comfortable that I started getting in bed with him with my pants pulled down to my ankles. Not completely undressed but undressed just enough to move up a level giving him the step he needed to go farther. My fear that his mother or someone walking in on us stayed close in my thoughts, but not close enough to keep me from going along with the game.

We continued to play our game becoming more at ease, because we had not been caught.

The afternoon when we were busted in the mist of doing the oochie coochie, we both froze, in shock and had no idea what was going to happen. He was on top of me and we were in a major trouble. His mother beat us out of the bed with her hands. Grabbing me by the back of my shirt, she headed toward her bedroom for a belt. She whipped my ass out the door of her house into the door of ours and right into another beating from my mother.

I wasn't sure how bad his beating was, he claimed it was nothing but my ass beating stuck firmly in my head, but it was not long before I was back next door and playing some house games again, never got caught again either.

In revealing my experiences of the sexual behaviors and how curious they made me about what went on behind closed doors with adults, I have to share an event that still tickles me pink to this day.

While in this same little two bedroom, one bath brick house with red and white porch and window covers, I would split open my forehead and carry that scar to this day. One of the men my mother fooled around with was a police officer. His time at our house was on a regular basis and he spent time playing with me when he came around. He had a dog as big as a horse and I mainly enjoyed riding his dog's back.

On one afternoon, he was at the house and they were in the bedroom handling grown folk's business. I took full advantage of my mother's preoccupation, and lost my mind. I jumped from couch to couch, across the table and somewhere in the midst, slipped to the floor banging my head on the corner of the coffee table.

I screamed for dear mercy as the blood blinded my right eye. They ran out fixing their clothes…*yes I never missed a beat, even in pain I saw it all.* He ran out to his car to bring in a first aid kit to bandage me up and off to the hospital we went. He took me to the hospital in his police car.

With a sucker in my mouth, we moved through traffic with the siren on as if I had suffered a life-threatening injury…I smiled the whole ride feeling important.

Once at the hospital and I seeing the needle and thread, I did not feel so important anymore. I felt more like losing my mind again. The tears were on and I was acting crazy as hell. Refusing to cooperate, they had to hold me down so the doctor could stitch me up. Putting that needle in my head gave me a phobia for needles from that day forward.

Now every time I have to deal with needles this event flashes across my mind and I realize how attentive I was to the activities in my environment at a young age.

Finding the Courage to Fight Back

First let me repeat that this is just the beginning, and no, I'm not telling everything. I am giving a glimpse of my experiences to allow you to understanding of what I was shown in my early years.

During our conversation and walk through the sequels of my story I will talk about how these events shaped my behaviors in ways not healthy for a young girl. These events would take me to places unimaginable and not to mention how quickly....so let's keep on walking.

We are going to sit between the ages four and six because my memories are not clear on an exact age or the exact years. There were so many events happening in my life, happening and happening at the speed of light. For some reason, not too many of these events were happy or positive.

I do not know why or how all these negative and hurting experiences were never suppressed in my mind. I learned the difference between men and women, vaginas and penises, the fundamentals of sex acts *both physically and visually*, violent arguments, and the effects.

To be honest, no one gave a damn about what was seen or heard, or maybe they were too busy to pay attention.

On to the next seed and how some of the ones already embedded sprouted…with what I had already experienced I was ready to do some fighting back.

The next time I had to encounter my stepbrother we were living in another house. This house had unforgettable features.

I remember we could sit in the front yard and watch movies playing on the nearby drive-in movie screens. This house also provide a unique shape, at least it was for me because I could run non-stop around a wall to keep my stepbrother away.

The activities with my older stepbrother came back to haunt my much more developed mind. It did not take long for his need to fondle me to return

I am sitting here laughing now but back then it was on and I spent a lot of evenings running in a circle around that wall.

We were in school together by this encounter at School 74; I believe I was in kindergarten. My baby brother took pictures with me at school that same year but he was in day care. My stepbrother and I had to walk to school together. During those walks he kept up his torturing me with those *'half-breed'* comments. Half-breed was the choice word in the streets.

Along with these memories there are several more from this time that stuck with me.

Encountering my stepbrother is top of the list and this time I was prepared. Even with my exposure to sex and the events I did participate in with the boy next door, I just could not understand how my stepbrother wanted to do the nasty with me. Did he not realize I was his stepsister?

Not by blood, but through our baby brother and family interaction? *No joke, that boy refused to give up and was determined to make me do what he wanted.*

One evening in particular, our parents had just walked out the door and the chase began. Around and around the wall we went. As soon as my stepbrother doubled back to catch me, he knocked me to the floor on the kitchen side. *I thought I was smart, I did not think about him changing directions.* The door opened; ha, ha I thought in my mind.

His ass was busted trying to screw me.

My vocabulary was growing, oochie coochie was out and screwing was the new word. Hell, he was on top of me but I was in trouble too. They told us to sit on the couch until they returned. My stepbrother for the first time was so scared of what our father was going to do to us that he left me alone.

Then the front door opened again. Our eyes met, filled with fear. The outcome in my mind was, *it's over.* I had to sit on the couch for hours so I felt this was my punishment.

Little did I know it was not over for me yet! After questioning us, and with me telling on my stepbrother, I got my butt whipped too. I was pissed and ready to get revenge on my stepbrother by any means necessary.

A couple of nights went by and my stepbrother was scheming again. This time he had a new plan of action to sucker me in. If he only knew, I was wiser now and had seen much more since our last encounter.

When he snuck into my room waking me and telling me to come see, I immediately took offense to him. He grabbed my arm and dragged me to the hall.

I knew once we entered the hall that he was on another mission besides trying to get freaky with me. We turned out of my room heading toward our parents' door. There was something he was dying to show me. I already had seen this "something"… our parents having sex.

I used this opportunity to try to get him in trouble by pushing the door open. It didn't work; they were too into each other to hear the squeak. Taking off, my stepbrother ran back into his room and stayed the remainder of the night.

That boldness from me somehow helped me. My stepbrother stopped physically messing with me. *Yes, I mean it just like I said it!* He did continue to make fun of my mixed heritage and he went as far as to get the other kids in the neighborhood to talk about me too.

He began to use silly ways to get back at my ass. He would make me walk alone to school in the snow, knowing I really did not know my way and when that didn't satisfy him he would terrorize me in my sleep.

Me, I had no choice but to find ways to defend myself and maintain some sense of sanity. I cursed him out and the kids that made fun of me. I started getting him in trouble by telling our parents about him coming into my room and messing with me at night, not that it made him stop. He just continued as if he needed that satisfaction from treating me the way he did.

One morning while walking to school, he left the house before me intentionally so I would have to walk alone. This morning was very cold.

I can visualize this morning as if it was yesterday and let me tell you it is funny.

I left the house and knew it would take forever to get to school because I had to find my way. I made several wrong turns. Cutting around the corner, I ran into my stepbrother.

He was talking to a girl. Once he noticed me, he must have had something smart to say because the girl pushed him backward and walked away. He laughed and told me he was not walking to school with me so go away! I replied, it was cold and I would get lost before finding my way and he laughed.

The girl walked into her house and came out with an umbrella. Clearly she knew my troubles. She told me if I got cold walking to school, open the umbrella and use it to block the wind from blowing directly at me. She even drew me a map to guide me to school.

With her help, I had a way to stay warm on that walk to school. With every block, I kneeled down in the middle of the street and used the umbrella for shelter like an igloo.

Slowly but surely I was learning to deal with my stepbrother, his dirty ways and my attention faded from him…on to the other events happening around our house.

One event in particular was being introduced to gun play. I had seen guns by now, but I had not witnessed one being fired. One evening, not too sure what caused the commotion but our father was shot at in the front yard. Everyone was hollering, screaming and just plain losing it.

I can remember our parents talking while standing in the front yard, and a car drove up. There were words passed between the adults. When the car sped off, the bullets rang.

We were told to go into the house and stay. Shortly after more words between our parents, our father got his gun and left. What came of that, I cannot remember. This event sticks out the most because it caused me to have a fear of guns and it took me years to shake that fear.

One other event that never left my thoughts was the nightmare about a gorilla. This nightmare stuck with me over the years. For so long I couldn't figure out what it meant, *I will talk about what I found that dream to mean for me at a later time in another sequel of my story.* The dream was scary.

I was awakened by a big black gorilla, this was real to me…*my eyes where open* and he was chasing me around in my bed cornering me against the wall. I remember kneeling in the bed crying with my hands covering my eyes. Suddenly I jumped, standing in the middle of the bed and screaming at the top of my lungs…"Leave me alone, go away".

I blinked and he was gone. I never forgot the glare in that gorilla's eyes.

I stood in the middle of my bed with my hands on my hips, booty out, my neck extended forward and yelling at the top of my voice to defeat him. I can still see the confusion on my stepfathers face when he ran through the door to see what I was yelling about.

Family Drama

For one reason or another, we were always moving, staying with family or family was staying with us. During most of that family-to-family living I was next to my favorite uncle and aunt.

Being around those two was the bomb for me. My aunt, *my natural mother's sister* and my uncle *my natural father's brother,* treated me as if I was their child. Living with them gave me the opportunity to be treated like I was a child.

I always looked at them as to be my real parents. They showed real love for me.

People that saw us together constantly complimented our relationship, telling us how beautiful we looked together. My uncle, to me, took up the slack for my father and never left my side.

I love and will never stop loving him and hate he is no longer with me here on earth. I do know he will always be with me in spirit...

My aunt claimed me as her daughter and gave me the love I missed from my mother. They had their problems as a couple and my uncle was a real trip all the time. He was a handful for anyone to deal with.

Being with them a lot meant I was always in the middle of their drama, the arguing and fighting during their ups and downs. However, regardless of their mess when I messed up they would bail me out no matter how bad it was.

Now that I have expressed my love for them I will put their pieces together to how they fit in this puzzled life of mines.

We lived under the same roof during several periods of my childhood; therefore, when we weren't under the same roof it felt like we were. I was always observing the way they showed love for each other and with all their fighting I saw how destructive their love was too.

My aunt was just as much a handful to deal with. They fought like cats and dogs, day in and day out.

Because of their feelings for me, I was constantly around and in the center of them fighting. My presence didn't make a difference when they were mad. My uncle would still kick off in my aunt's ass. Scared and fighting for her life, my aunt would always manage to get away and get help.

My uncle would not stick around, before she could return, he would scoop me up making his way to the car.

We would ride for hours, non-stop. With me on the armrest, close to his side, my uncle would explain in a quiet voice what I had witnessed. He'd tell me these episodes between him and my aunt were grownup problems, also trying to explaining why the fights were happening.

He schooled me as much as he saw fit. After every episode, I got a present to pamper my tears…like my first bubblegum machine.

With them being in my life the way they were, my uncle was by my side when I first experienced a female conning me into skipping school so that she could make a move on me. He was also by my side when I stole for the first time and started displaying my tomboyish behaviors.

These events went like this…

My aunt and uncle were always kicking off an argument over anything. The argument I hold close was the first time I was the reason for their fight. This fight ties all the above experiences together so let's roll.

A couple of houses down, a lil white girl was interested in me. Not as a friend, but a g-i-r-l-f-r-i-e-n-d.

One morning as we left the house, she talked me into coming to her house to play for a while. In her room, she hooked my ass with the notion that if we stayed inside the house we would not have to go to school. No one would know and we would have fun. Down for fun, I agreed.

She wanted to play house *only this play scene had two mommies and no daddy.* The babe was very experienced; she did not hesitate and wanted to go straight to having sex. *A sex that was not new in my mind, but I hadn't experienced it physically.* She kissed me and started to rub on me. At the blink of an eyelash her lil ass was taking off her clothes.

I froze. Then she pissed me off by laughing and calling me scared. Jumping around like a chicken, she exposed her lil white ass and looked as crazy as I did watching. Running out of her house crying, I cut around the bushes and ran right into the arms of my uncle.

The surprised look on his face due to seeing me at home and not in school made me cry even harder. I could tell my uncle anything, and yes, I told him everything. I don't think he really knew how to explain what happened between me and that lil white girl, but he gave it a shot. His explanation for her behavior didn't make it seem so bad. By him telling my lil curious ass it wasn't that bad, didn't help the situation. It just made me wonder more.

After our discussion, he got on my ass about skipping school. By the end of the scolding, he still covered for me. I stayed with him the remainder of the day, cutting corners and hanging out that was *his daily routine*. We returned home as if he had picked me up from school.

He did lay down the rules from earlier again before we got out of the car; #1 I had to stay away from that lil girl's house, #2 I could not play with her outside, and #3 if I ever skipped school again it wouldn't be pretty. I knew exactly what that meant. I cooled out and really didn't have a problem with his rules just yet.

We will return to his rules later.

Now let's talk about my tomboyish behaviors and how my boyish ways would put my uncle in the midst of a fight amongst kids one afternoon. I loved being around the boys and doing what they felt a girl could not do. That was one of my ways to get attention.

Not realizing how messy boys could be too, one evening after school I had to climb the tree with the boys to prove myself. This tree had a clubhouse at the top that was held up by several branches.

Accompanying the group of boys I was with, there was one smart mouth nigga. He was always talking smack about someone. This day that *someone* was me. He lived on our street and the commotion at my house never stayed inside, giving him the fuel to start a fire with me. He knew a lil too much of our business.

He opened his mouth talking out the side of his neck about the fights between my aunt and uncle, and it made me mad. Before I could think I was all over his ass, swinging like a wild lil girl and screaming all sorts of profanity. We were on a sidewalk fighting next to a wire gate.

Somehow, in the swing of things my eyebrow got cut on the gate and blood was flowing everywhere. Scaring the hell out of me and the boys watching, one of them ran for help. He returned with my uncle to stop the fight.

Once I received some first aid attention, I was ready for more and had to go back to the tree house. The boy I fought acted as if everything was cool, and helped me up the tree. I came with an agenda and needed revenge. Once in the clubhouse I maneuvered myself close to him and started a tussle again. Again, I was the one left in tears. This time I landed at the bottom of the tree after our struggle.

My uncle had to return to my rescue and by now he was pissed. I sat holding my arm and crying. Stubborn as hell, I got back in the tree and was determined to see this lil boy hurt.

I felt like crap once I got my revenge, because he broke a bone when he hit the ground. Yep, he did fly like an eagle out of that tree and in the back of my mind I kind of had that taste of sweet revenge too. His bone healed and our relationship did too.

With all the sneaking to get what I wanted, up to this point, I had never gotten caught. The first time I stole a pack of *Now and Later* candy from the store I got in a heap of mess, more than having those *Now and Later* candy was worth. I even remember the flavor...banana!

The embarrassment was not cool at all. My mother was so mad she demanded that I go back to the store and return the candy.

Yeah right, I'm home now...I thought.

My mother was the one to bust me; my uncle was the one that took me back to the store. I gave the candy back and apologized to the man at the register. My uncle talked more mess than a lil on the way home.

He was more pissed about taking me back to the store than me stealing the candy. Later that night my uncle handed me a pack of *Now and Later* candy, banana flavor. I laughed and wondered when did he buy that candy?

He did not buy them when we were at the store; he stole them and told me *"what momma doesn't know won't hurt her"*. I was all for that.

Let's bring these episodes together and how I was the cause of a fight between my aunt and uncle. All hell hit the fan because my uncle was too easy on me when I misbehaved. With him not being tuff enough with me, I seemed to get into even more trouble.

My aunt was somewhat jealous of the relationship my uncle and I developed. She felt I was hardheaded and never learned my lesson *she was right*, and she knew my uncle was the reason I did not learn from those mistakes.

Already mad at my uncle and me, I tossed more fuel to the flame and took my ass back over to the lil white girl's house to pick up where we left off. Now I thought I was ready, I should have taken my ass to school.

Her mother caught us playing our mommy game and it was on. Her mother snatched me up by my arm and marched me home to talk to my aunt. As we approached the front door, I noticed everyone was already mad and coming out of the house geared up.

I figured they were headed to find me. This had to be the only reason everyone was home that time of day and at the same time. The school had called both our parents because we did not show up that morning.

My ass was in deeper than I could imagine. After their talk about us getting caught in a sexual act, I got chewed out about skipping school. My uncle felt he had to make me understand how my behavior was unacceptable. Unfortunately, he ran his mouth a bit too much.

While cursing me out about me returning to the lil girl's house, his words caught my aunt's attention. In her reaction to the knowledge of our secret, she responded quickly as she turned her body towards him and the boiling process began. Listening to him tell on us both, she hauled off and slapped the holy crap out of him. Her mouth flew open and the real deal was in full affect.

My uncle really wasn't tripping. He realized he was wrong and accepted the slap. My aunt demanded he would be the one to whip me. Boy was I glad for that, I knew my uncle couldn't do it and I felt safe and ready for the beating. My aunt stuck her head in the door and I was hollering as if my uncle was tearing flesh. *Hilarious I know!* Now try to imagine the look on her face when seeing him brutalizing the pillow and not me.

The fight was on…my aunt always had to turn into a "Billy Badass", and be the one to throw the first lick. That mouth of hers would make things even worse. My uncle beat her something serious, like always, but this time I felt like …(can't find a word) because of it. Thinking, why didn't I follow the rules?

Regardless of how bad I was, I never liked to see them fight, and I especially didn't want them fighting because of me.

Comfort of the Streets

B eing in the middle of family drama and not caring for the pain they inflicted on one another, I began to search for a way out. My curiosity of what the streets had to offer began to interest me more.

I found a sense of safety and freedom and in no time it overwhelmed me.

Ms. Fast Ass and running alongside of some cousins; I was introduced to the streets at a faster pace than I would have if they weren't there to teach me. There were both boys and girls interaction among these cousins.

Our mother played cards, and I mean played the whole night long! My aunt and my mother hung like two peas in a pot stuck at the bottom, not seeing the damage being passed into the minds of us younger kids.

For several years, we stayed close to them picking up on and learning everything we saw them do. We eventually used those experiences to survive. We had no choice but to be around all that negative behavior, so I personally adapted.

Our older cousins only stuck around long enough for my aunt and mother to leave and then they'd leave, leaving us to fend for ourselves *the younger kids*. Left at our aunt's for the night and sometime more than a night, I started hanging in the streets tuff. We had to stay out of the older kids' face or get knocked the hell down. I would vanish, messing around in the 'hood. *What hood? Hell, Indy has several and I've been in most of them.*

I can say that having the freedom of no supervision was not what I needed, but for the most part I enjoyed it. The nights around our cousins were always full of excitement.

The beginning stages of a world full of tragedy were yet to come. Hanging with them, I picked up stealing at a new level; because of being left to fend for myself I stole everything from candy to clothes.

I stayed in the neighborhood candy store, grocery stores and department store. I would walk for hours with nothing to do and nowhere to be. Knocking on people's doors and hanging at the corners that supplied the group of kids that stayed up to no good.

Remember the cousin that signed my ass earlier? She was a part of this family of cousins and she brought the world of prostitution into my picture of life as well as what the word really meant. White! Black! It didn't matter as long as they had green. Yep, M-O-N-E-Y! I would watch her get dressed for her dates. Spending time with her, she talked to me about how men used women and that if you stay on top of your game, how to use them back and get paid well.

For the longest time, she hid the fact that it wasn't only money she wanted but her addiction for drugs that made her go get that money.

After her rendezvous, she would come home messed up and talking crazy to everyone. Sometimes she'd even talk crazy all day and night. I realized her drug habit when she walked through the door early one morning bent over holding her stomach. She was having trouble breathing. Her eyes were bloodshot red and full of tears from the pain of her nightlife.

I remember this morning so clearly, because I was the only one awake to let her in and I had to dump the trashcan she vomited in to keep down the funk. I spent most of the morning keeping cold wet towels near her bedside and on her forehead. I thought she was going to die and she would not let me wake up anyone to help us.

She talked non-stop about her tricks and the drugs until she could not talk anymore, fading in and out of consciousness. My ears got full of her nightlife that morning.

From prostitution to gangs I lived for the excitement…but with fear.

My boy cousins were into the gang activities and I saw a lot of it first-hand. I recall blue and red the colors for the Vice Lords and Cripps, the gangs kicking up most of the crime around this time. The drugs, guns and violence became popular around their house.

These activities were so close that I felt danger with every breath I took. Most of the time I wondered which one of us would be hurt or maybe killed.

I talked to one of the older boys about my fear. Why I let him in on my feelings, only the Lord knows. Once I did, he made it his business to teach me how to defend myself, and he had his own methods.

I did not like his methods or the repercussions if I didn't do it his way. But I knew back then, as if it was today, why I had to be able to defend myself. Being in and around their house was never safe.

Let me elaborate on not safe…

Several nights would include one of my cousins running into the house bloody and busted up from the wars in the streets. Other nights involved everyone piled up in a closet or under the beds because of bullets headed towards or into the house.

Once the drama was over, the normal activities like drug sales and crap games would pick up. For us children, we would head back outside into the night playing hide–and-go-it. *Let your imagination give a meaning.*

There were several family fights daily around my cousin's house. *To me it was normal.* They were rough with no love for one another.

I recall walking up the alley hearing my aunt hollering her lungs out and a loud thump, as she was being bounced off the walls. The voice cursing at her told me the story of what to expect once I got closer. Approaching the back steps that lead to the yard, I saw the door open and the voices were clear with each word said.

As I walked up the sidewalk, my aunt's body was in sight and headed my way. Her body flew out the house to greet the cement at the bottom of the steps, knocking her unconscious, her eyelids were open and her eyeballs rolled in her head. She did survive and the scars did heal, but that would not be the last of it. The fights continued.

Actually, all the family-on-family fights were just as bad as if we were strangers.

Let me talk about our fights, the ones that included other cousins when they came over. My cousins made the younger kids fight one another and if we did not fight and fight hard, they would kick our ass and make us start all over. There were times when our consequences for not fighting or fighting hard were being beat by one of the older cousins.

Depending on which cousin it was, this would determine the extent of our punishment.

We might be beat with a belt, but most of the time the first was the weapon of choice. We were thrown, not pushed, down stairs and off rooftops. *It's not as bad as it sound; there always was a mattress below.* Our fear was their joy. We had to prove ourselves or suffer…d*umb, I know, oh well.* If we told, the ass kicking was not the only way to punish us.

We would be starved for the day to satisfy the older cousins who thought starving us would toughen us up, and stop us from tattling. It worked for me but pissed me off just that much more. I got to the point that my anger, when at my aunt's house would explode so I cursed and would fight their asses back. I was not taking any more ass whippings, at least not from them.

Yes I got mad and it was cute to them…so my cousins seen how bold I had become and how I was trying to fight back and the fight was really on.

Like the time we were living in a motel with them. For some reason, three of us did not go to school this day. One of my cousins got mad over a baloney sandwich and started arguing with me. Yep baloney was steak for us and came with a fight for the last piece. The last piece of boloney in the pack and two hungry nigga's!

My cousin and I were going head on for that piece. We cursed, pushed, and tussled to get to the dresser the package laid on. When my other cousin came out of the restroom, it got even uglier.

As my cousin defended me and fought with his brother, I got caught in the middle of their fight while they tussled on the bed. In the blink of an eye, my cousin who was defending me, fist went up and came down connecting with my nose.

With my blood already boiling from fighting, his fist connected with my nose caused my blood to splatter all over the place. My eyes got as big as a pair of balloons. I lost my mind on both of their asses, swinging crazy and not caring about getting hurt at that point. Once they got me calmed down and cleaned up, I ended up with the last piece of baloney.

From that day on I didn't have to prove myself, at least not to those two. I fought first, and never asked questions. By now I was numb and didn't' care.

I can go on and on about the events and trauma I experienced and saw being around these cousins, but I think I will let it be. Our time did not end there. It did pick back up later. Hell, these days gave me what I needed in order to survive the days ahead. I learned their ways quickly, but I didn't need to see or experience it at my age. But I did!

Before I move on…let me tell ya the thought that just entered my head…while traveling down my dramatized life of memories, my brain is like a prison. The door is never closed….continuously revolving, with more bull returning from the outside world, as I become more and more involved in my memories.

Curious & Nosey

During the time when my mother didn't have a man under the same roof, momma had her hands in some of everything and most of the time, everyone, as well as their business.

In those days, bikers and strip clubs and it was on and poppin', so was momma.

On momma's nights out she would leave us in the care of whoever would watch us or any family member who would put up with us.

But when she couldn't find a sitter, she took us to the parties she attended. I witnessed some interesting things at those parties. Bikers were like family with their own culture and parties where held on a regular basis. The gatherings would be at one of the member's house and accompanied with activities that children should not see.

I remember being at a party over one of the members house. This house was two stories and the yard was near an alley. They had a barrel fire and people everywhere. All the kids that came were sent upstairs.

There were three other kids with a mindset similar to mine *nosey, if I recall it correctly* and we did not stay upstairs in the rooms for long. We would sneak around watching the adults as they partied.

Party they did. I saw the drugs they used from smoking weed to snorting cocaine. . *Weed was not new to me, I had hit several joints.* There was even the needle in the arm of a man slouched over sitting on the toilet with his arm across the sink. *At that time that was unfamiliar to me, his habit was new to my eyes.*

I watched more than one adult couple having sex in several areas of the living room, *doing their thang.* There were women with women sexual scenes, two women one man, and two men one woman... sucking pussy, blowing dick. Sex acts, I know today to be orgies! There was no one there telling me I was too young to watch. I wanted to see it all and every chance I got I peeked.

These experiences put the icing on the cake for me what more was there to know about sex? For me, not much more could be seen. At least not until later down the road... Let's keep on keepin' on.

Project Life

I learned a hell of a lesson living in the Meadows, a housing project in Indianapolis. Life was crazy in a good way and wild as hell, I can honestly say, "Those were the days".

Momma was smoking weed, partying and had it going on in my sight. Our apartment was on the ground level of Meadow Drive. The living room ceiling was decorated by hanging a fishnet and putting the record covers in it.

The red light set it off. This room was amazing to me, especially when I was buzzed.

I would steal weed from my momma's stash and one of my cousins would roll it up, yep, one from the ruthless crew and off to the cut the corner we went. The area behind the red and white building on the corner of Meadow Dr. and 38th was our hide out and get high spot.

Momma was on the go all the time. When she was home, she had company or was high. She never realized what I was doing or into. She only paid attention when it came down to me embarrassing her.

Embarrassing for her was the day I ran home crying. She tried to uphold this tuff woman crap and expected me to follow suit.

This day she was entertaining a friend and my cousin was there my earlier ass signer. This friend of hers was the bomb to her and she was on that money hunt using me as the bait. Fancy in yellow was my name for him. He drove one of the prettiest, yellow, old school cars around. And when he gave me a ride in that car, I felt beautiful.

Anyway, back to how I ended up running in the house crying and embarrassing her. I never had luck with having female friends. The only interest the girls in my 'hood had in me was daring each other to kick my ass. I guess they figured the boys would not hang around me anymore if they beat me up…since boys seem to be the reason for most of my fights with girls.

After the hell I face with my cousins, I got tired of running and crying that had to change. For some odd reason I never faced one person at a time these girls always ganged up to fight me; however, my breakthrough did show itself and I had several girls surrounding me. They were ready to jump me. I was a fighter, but I wasn't the one to challenge more than one at a time.

Let me brag, one of them could not hang with me, but two was too many. I hadn't quite dealt with fighting on that level yet. Looking back, momma's luck with women wasn't any better.

I explained to my mother what was going to happened with these chicks, if they caught me outside. I even made it a point to tell her how many there was, a lot! She promptly sent me back outside to fight those girls. She told me I better beat every girl involved and if I came back and had not, she would beat me and send me back out again.

What?

I was mad as hell and what was I going to do now?

Thinking, this woman is crazy as hell, there is no way I was fighting all those girls with no help, not me. I would have preferred to take an ass beating from momma if I felt that would be the end, at least for that day.

But her statement was clear. The girls and momma kicking my ass, was too much, just too much.

To hell with that, I thought. I stayed out of sight from the girls, hiding in an empty apartment and playing with a cat and her kittens.

Hours passed and while on my way in to brag on how I beat on those girls the best I could. Tearing my shirt and messed up my hair to make my story believable…I looked up and one of the girls was coming up the sidewalk. This chick had a flip lip and was the ringleader of the crew.

As we passed one another she giggled and I lost it. Turning around grabbing her by the back of her head gave me an advantage.

She never expected me to fight. We rolled and swung for minutes, and once she started pleading I was relieved. I was ready for the fight to be over, but I really thought the next day would get worse.

I figured she would have her crew beat the hell out of me. Surprising they didn't. Instead, they actually didn't mess with me anymore. We never really even spoke again even when our paths crossed.

The lesson I learned from this experience was simple…Fight the person that had the most to say and the rest would probably not want to fight at all. I also refused to tell my mother about my conflicts with females.

Used As Bait

My mother had a way of keeping a man around and most of the time I was her tool to do so.

This started very early in my childhood and didn't stop. She ran through so many men (probably before and after my conception). Only God knows how many and the number of encounters I had with them.

My father missed out on my childhood. He felt being in my life meant he would have to provide for me. He wasn't prepared to do that so he stayed far away. I wanted him around to guide and help mold me in some fashion. Every time I saw him, his ass was on the run. His brother was there for me most of my life and made it a little easier to deal with. To be honest, I do not have any bad memories of my relationship with my father so I guess that's good.

I struggled with his absence and wanted to know why. Only to be left empty with my thoughts to find the answer. Those answers I so desperately wanted faded with ever empty promise he made. Promise after promise to come around, I eventually learned to stop hanging on to the lies he told me. I held on to the love for my father through my relationship with my uncle. This way he always stayed close to my heart. Time gave me a better understanding of who my father was. Somehow, I even found a way to justify his actions and why he wasn't around.

Yes time gave me a better understanding, but it also brought confusion. The lies that rolled from my mother's lips made it hard to deal with feeling anything resembling fatherly love…even from afar.

My mother used me to keep her men and money available by allowing others to claim me as their daughter. And all those fools made me think they believed I was their daughter, or maybe they thought being with my mother was all that. *Who knows?* I do know they all played her game.

She would tell different men that they were my father. I would have to interact with them, acting as a daughter. *Hell why not, my father did not want anything to do with me*, is the excuse I used. I had always been around my uncles and my father's brothers. I still felt unsure of my father, with all the bull how would I really know who was my biological father. Well I would say I knew but I just didn't give a damn anymore. Not to mention how Momma had my mind twisted up with all her lies she needed me to be her money maker!

A biracial child, for some black men was like hell yea! And everyone my mother cornered wanted to be that man. So I had about four different want to-be daddies in my face at one point or another. Once the money was gone, so were the men. But only one stayed for the long haul.

One of those men included me in his family. We would go on fishing outings or to the park with his other children. When my mother went dancing, I would stay at his mother's house. I was told this woman was my grandmother.

She was a sweet person and provided me with some experiences that still brings a smile to my face whenever I think of her. She had a beautiful home. I loved the feeling and smell of Caress soap on my skin, and oatmeal for breakfast every morning.

These pleasant memories have stayed with me throughout my life and they all started in her home.

This grandmother, *I had many grandmothers too,* would break my ass from pissing in the bed. One of her rules was for a little girl not to smell pissy early in the morning. The switch she used on my ass taught me to follow her rules and not drink water or anything before I went to bed. Damn, I still remember the tears I cried begging her to stop. That woman had power in that hand she used to swing that switch.

Claiming this father for me ended when momma felt it was time to move on to the next episode in her life, time to prey on another man from her past and a *"father"* for me.

My brother was lucky. In my opinion, his father was around from day one. He never had to pretend that a series of men was his "father". Our mother never used him in that way.

By the time I was five or six, a man that hung around at that time was named as another one of my fathers. He was a biker and showed a lot of interest in me when he was around. During this time in my life, I did not need any more confusion in my head. Unfortunately, my mother would start steer it up again. She had this man sit me down and ask me how I would feel if he told me he was my father.

Knowing the mess my mother is capable of starting, I just played along. He stuck around for a while.

He introduced me to his kids and then vanished from my life. I would too if I was in his shoes. I think he realized how much chaos was going on in my mother's life and he did not want to be a part of it.

Then came a real blast from the past a man who regardless of what my mother said or who I thought my father was, he wasn't going anywhere. I had heard several stories about this man that was named on my birth certificate.

He lived in Haughville with a woman he had been with for some time. I really never got along with her. As this father story goes…My mother hooked up with him in her fifth or six month of pregnancy. He wanted me to be his child so bad.

He wanted to believe that when I was born I was a premature baby at birth. This would mean he really could be my biological father. I do and will always claim him as my father. I have heard the war stories and the events I was placed in the middle of as a baby.

Destructive from birth…

There was the story about him being involved in a big drug ring. There were several attempts on his life, because of his clout in the game. I was told details about one of those attempts…this is what supposedly happened…*The house I spoke of was on Parker and is where they lived when I was born.*

My mother and this father were approached as they walked up the sidewalk to the house. A couple of masked men with guns forced them into the house. They were being robbed.

One of momma's lady friends saw or heard the mess that had started out front. She grabbed me from the couch I was laying on and got in a closet. She hid there with me until all was clear to come out. No one was hurt. There was some fighting and shooting involved. The robbers did not get any dope, only the money, purses and jewelry.

Like I said I was told...

This father was crazy and if put in the position, he would kill...let me talk about when he was put in that position.

This event would be more than a story told to me, most of this was in black and white for me to see the proof. The same year that I was born, my mother and a friend cranked up more mess with my stepfather. They did not realize the price to pay would be hell for someone. For some odd reason, my mother has always played with the minds of others as if she had nine lives to spare. This head game of hers put a man's head on the floor and her man's hands in cuffs.

My mother and her friend kicked it off. My mother and this father were arguing because my mother and her friend were up to no good and playing on the phone this day. After one too many calls and threats, my stepfather loaded up.

He put on a trench with a sawed off shotgun that had the barrel cut short, hanging around his shoulder by a rope. They drove to the house. He was looking to put a stop to their crap. He stood at the door of another man's house, with my mother standing beside him. My momma had me in her arms. My stepfather was prepared to kill or be killed.

Under his trench was that sawed off pump with his hands prepared to shoot. He had no fear of using it. As the arguing progressed between the four adults, the tempers got out of control. The man of the house split my stepfather's skull open with a machete while at the same time, the man had his head blown completely off his body by my stepfather's pump. My mother and I were covered in the blood from both men.

I can only imagine watching stupid and ugliness unfold would affect someone for life. It obviously never affected my mother because she is still the cause of much more mess.

My stepfather was arrested and spent five years in jail. He never forgave my mother for causing him so much pain and suffering. After she got tired of being around, she left him in jail. His biggest problem with her was taking me out of his life the way she did. In the beginning of his time spent in jail, he watched from the windows of the Marion County Jail as I learned to walk.

Momma would walk me up and down the sidewalk for him to see, but the day came when he had to imagine me outside the window walking for him. Momma was moving on. Years would pass before he reentered my life.

He was out of my life when I really needed a father to step-up to the plate for my well-being, but he did find his way into my heart years later. *With my daddy drama off my chest and out of the way, let's move on.*

Shattered Mind

The first taste of what her next couple of years would hold was introduced to my mother early in this particular hookup. The fights would be real bad ass kicking's for my mother and me followed, from here on out. I remember the beginning of the fear this man instilled in us.

To this very day, I can still feel the fear as if it was happening at this very moment. They were arguing about my aunt *the one from earlier that was married to my uncle that protected me* and we were told to go upstairs.

For as long as I can remember there was always fighting between my parents, aunts, uncles, cousins, and just about anybody else that was around. The ass kicking's really got a hold of me. I was aware of what to expect, but was still too young to help myself.

No, I did not know what we were in for, until that day came. Let me say, I knew he was the wrong man for my mother. I felt it straight from my soul the first step he took through the front door of the apartment where it all began.

This night I ran down the stairs towards the small restroom chasing my mother's screams. I came down the stairs, running toward her voice to find her hemmed against the wall in the restroom. He had his large hands around her neck, tears streaming down her face, *like a child prepared for an ass whipping.* I heard the fear of death in her cries for help.

My mouth hit the floor and my eyes grew big as saucers, instantly filling with tears when I stopped in my tracks at the edge of the door. I looked at my mother's small- frame body dangling in the air. She called my name and he turned only his head looking over his shoulder.

In a hard and deep tone, he hollered at me. He told me to "go back upstairs and don't come back down."

Returning upstairs, my little brother was sitting Indian-style in the floor of our mother's bedroom. His face flushed red. His beautiful big round, brown eyes were filled with crocodile tears, showing the true length of his eyelashes. He blinked to empty the load trickling down his cheeks. He wasn't old enough to understand what was happening to our mother.

He only wanted me to comfort him, which helped him to stay calm. I did not want him to be upset, so I just put my arms around him and held him in my arms as tight as I could. Covering his ears, I did not want him to hear the loud noises from our mother's body being pounded into the wall below us. I was not sure of what to do so I started praying and somehow we were able to fall asleep in the midst of our fear.

When the next morning arrived, I prayed that the monster in our home would be gone. That prayer was not answered, nor could I see him leaving in the near future. Not only was he still in our house, but he was on the warpath and looking to complete his mission from the night before.

My aunt apparently had borrowed some money and did not pay him back when she guaranteed he would get his money. Our mother wouldn't be the only one to deal with his anger.

He packed our asses into the car and headed to Fort Harrison. He was out to get my aunt's ass now. When we got to my aunt's job, my brother and I were told to stay in the car. I watched him grip my mother's arm as they marched towards the door of the building.

Not being able to see what was taking place inside; my mind was praying to see the police pull up at any minute. *Nope, that did not happen.* The officers working at Fort Harrison escorted them out of the building.

Back in the car, my mother was being hollered at, taking the heat for what my aunt failed to do...pay this monster his money. We sat in the back and did not make a sound. Listening to how he jacked up my aunt by her neck, we learned this was the reason they were escorted out of the building.

All I could think about was how my mother and brother's father would settle their arguments. I had witnessed some horrible scenes of violent fights, but up to this point none included our mother.

Their fights had not been this violent. They did get rough. But there was a difference between the first fight I witnessed between my mother and brother's father to the ones between the monster and my mother.

I could only imagine how bad it would be the next time my mother and her newfound man would crank up the volume. Not long after this incident, I learned just how bad the fights would get. How bad it would be for me as well?

My mother did not leave this man. After that ass kicking, it was like my mother fell in love. *Sick, I know!* She allowed this man to stay around and things only got more violent. They argued damn near every day and I waited for him to beat the hell out of her again and again. He knew what he was doing.

After the first fight, he held his composure and moved in for the kill slowly. He waited to have her in the position he needed so she would depend on him. Because my mother was so money hungry, it didn't take long to get her totally dependent on him. She allowed this man to stay in our house.

She convinced my brother and me that he would never hit her again. She even wanted us to believe that he was extremely good to her. I really was not trying to hear it; all I wanted was for him to leave.

But my voice was never heard!

With no regard for how we felt, our mother up and moved us into this damn fool's apartment. I was in elementary school and they felt I was old enough to be home alone after school so I was given a key.

I came home after school one afternoon to a missing floor model television with no one home. Instantly, I knew there was going to be hell. With all the fights and arguments I had witnessed by now, my mind went into defense mode. I tried like hell to make myself believe they must have taken the television to be repaired. But the reality was; I was only trying to convince myself it was that simple. A useless thought because my stomach warned me otherwise!

Unsure of what to do, I laid on the floor between the twin beds of the room I shared with my brother. I used a coloring book to keep my mind occupied. Deep down inside I knew I had a reason to be scared…and I was and I began to silently pray. The fear of why the television was gone made coloring impossible, so I mentally worked on a plan.

I examined the window in the room. Mentally measuring the height of the wooden fence that enclosed the back patio, I wondered if I could get over it and get help without being caught. I made myself believe that I was bold enough to make a run for it. I seriously felt I could bring myself to run for help.

With my plan to flee for help in place, I laid and waited to hear the turn of the doorknob. Wondering, *Lord what would happen if they don't have the television?* The doorknob turned shortly after my stomach began to calm down, sending me back into an uncomfortable fear.

I took several deep breaths in order to prepare my body to move and then I heard a giant roar from him, "Tonie, bring your ass here, who the hell did you let into my house?"

Jumping to my feet, I looked toward the window. I hesitated on one hand, and on the other hand I had no doubt about the answer to my question, *did they take the television to the repair shop?* With that question he yelled out, the answer was definitely, No! This was starting to turn into a mystery that I would be expected to solve. I walked into the living room with my head down, stomach turning and scared as hell. I was not ready to face what was coming my way. His voice shook my soul and I knew where this situation was headed.

Approaching the entry of the living room, I could see him grabbing my mother. He was pushing her to the center of the room, away from the door. My brother had been with them; he was standing there looking as if he was about to for real booboo on himself, stiff as a board. Then another bone shaking roar filled the room as my brother was ordered to the bedroom with authority.

Once his head turned and his eyes shifted to me, I quietly answered him, "Didn't you and momma take the television to be repaired?" His face flared as he responded, "Don't f**king play with me. You are going to tell me who the hell was in my house!" The overwhelming fear inside of my mother came out and she began to beg, pleading with him to calm down a little. Knowing that would piss him off more, I stood looking at the scene praying even harder.

He told me to get my ass out of his face, so back into the bedroom I went. The loud roar of his arguing was on. It seemed like his mouth was releasing a roar that sent chills down my spine. Shock filled my soul as I stood looking at my brother's blank face. I looked past him, through the window and at the wooden fence. Through that window that I so desperately wanted to climb out to get help. I was full of fear, and did not dare move toward the window.

Thinking only of what would happen if I got caught trying to escape. I observed what I could from my bed to see what he was going to do to my mother. With a wall in the way I only heard the arguing. Knowing he had a clutch on my mother, I stood up from my bed in hopes to see more but greeted his face walking into the hallway. *Damn, I am in trouble now,* is all I could think. I knew he would mother sucker because I was off my bed, being noise and looking toward the living room.

Slam! The door was shut in my face. Stiffness came over both my brother and I. We could hear the pleading of my mother's voice and the thumps of her body being tossed from wall to wall around the house. He was beating the hell out of our mother. Her crying got louder and louder and so did his slapping and fussing.

Thankfully the first round was coming to an end. Several words were spoken in a semi-silent voice coming from my mother and right after the front door opened and slammed. The house was quiet, which seemed like forever. We didn't dare open the door of our bedroom. The thought of running for help entered my mind again, but now he was outside. Where out there was he? Knowing he was outside only made me fearful of going outside for help, so I just sat in the corner of the bed holding my brother.

The apartment door opened letting me know they were back. Grabbing my pillow, filling up inside with anger as my heart fluttered in fear, I listened to my mother talking to someone other than him. I realized she was on the phone, and I prayed she could get us help. Seconds later, there was a knock at the door. A sigh of relief came over me, thinking we would be saved.

While I listened from my room, I could make out what seemed to be the explanation for the missing television. Not real help after all. I hoped this information would cause him to go through his normal plea of forgiveness, giving my mother another day to live.

My name was called and I opened the door to answer quickly in order to keep him from getting more upset with me. The mess in the living room looked like the remnants of the damage left from a tornado, filling my vision of what my mother endured in the room. My heart rate increased from my seeing the condition of the living room.

Peeking from the corner of the wall that ended the hallway and entered the opening to the living room, I could see my mother. She was on the floor between his legs with her life in his hands. My eyes filled with tears again. He was sitting on the coffee table with the phone receiver in his hand. My mother apologized to me for being blamed for the missing television.

Now the answer he demanded me to supply earlier had an explanation. At that instant, I could tell she was seeking calmness from him and hoping me standing before the scene of what had happened would give him a reason to not continue the fighting. It wasn't going to work. By now his drive to finish was all I could see in his eyes.

The second round was on and it would include me. There is no telling what was in his head. He carried a rage that was uncontrollable. At this point, I could not understand why, even though beating on my mother was the only thing that seemed to satisfy him.

This time when the fighting kicked off we had the violence in view, as he beat our mother throughout the house, slamming her body into every wall in the house. He walked her through the apartment with one hand around her neck and punching her with his other hand. He pounded her head with his fist one minute. Seconds later he was pounding her head into the floor. In between the pounding, it seems he tried choking life from her body.

My mother's blood was splattered on every wall of every area of room in the apartment. He cursed and fussed about nothing that really mattered while he beat her to a pulp. Right in view from our bedroom, he slammed my mother on the hard hallway floor. I could not see her surviving this beating. Her body hit the floor with such force, that I felt she would surely die.

He pinned her body to the floor, pounding his fist into her face not giving a damn that we were watching. The fact that we were watching didn't even seem to bother him one bit.

He appeared to crave another adrenaline rush as he snatched me off the bed and dragged me toward the front of the apartment. He stepped over my mother as she grabbed the wall for support to pull herself up. Just as his foot touched back down, my body was slung.

From the opening of the hallway to the living room, my tiny ass flew across the room and landed on the coffee table. My body slid the full length of the table and came to a stop as my head crashed into the entertainment center. He picked me up from behind by my shirt and dragged me to the restroom backwards. I lay on my back looking at the ceiling hopelessly.

Before I could catch my breath, I was hemmed into the wall next to the restroom and he began to talk crazy.... saying things like, *my mother was the reason he acted out in this way.* I would think, *okay but where do I fit in?* I knew this was only his excuse for his actions. I clung to the sweet feeling of relief, but I still couldn't help but wonder what had I done to deserve this treatment? Releasing my body from the wall, he punched me. He hit me so hard in the face that I landed in the restroom on the floor face up.

How, I am not sure, but I ended up against the white clothes hamper with my legs straddling the toilet. Focusing my vision, my eyes fixed on his face and I realized I was in between his legs. He was on the toilet over me, slapping me and talking in a deep, scary voice. Folding his hand, those slaps became punches. He held me with one hand by my shirt, cutting off my wind, and causing me to cough from the tight grip he had on my shirt around my neck. Barely breathing, I received every punch he threw.

Fading in and out of consciousness, I recall opening my eyes, looking up at my mother. She had her back to me but I could see her face in the mirror. The water was running in the sink. She was running water on a rag she was going to use on her face. The reflection of her face in the mirror gave me no reason to believe we would live. The damage of what he had done to her was that bad. She was already discolored and swollen. My mother's posture was in such a slump as she stood there. I could tell he had really injured her.

I prayed for him to stop, hoping he would see how bad my mother was hurt and just leave. I really knew inside that we were by no means going to survive this time. We had no chance; our lives were nearing the end!

He continued to beat the dog crap out of me. I was so traumatized. His words began to sound like a foreign language in my head. I was unable to understand a word he said, as I laid there lifeless. The tears from my eyes had all drained out and I couldn't produce anymore. My body was in so much pain.

This must have insulted his ego, because he grabbed me as my mother screamed... "No!"

What was I going to do? Fight back? It wasn't my fault I had no more tears to shed! He hollered "your ass"... and before his sentence was complete...my ass was slammed into a closet door in the hall.

My feet dangled. My head was stuck in the hole made from the force of my body being slammed. He held me in place around my neck with one hand. My mother held his other arm in the air behind his head in my view. His fist was balled and meant to connect with my face.

My mother saved me from that punch. He let me go. My body fell to the floor and the blood drained from my head covering my face. Picking me up, my mother held on to me guiding me to my bed. My body just flopped, meeting the mattress in need of medical aid. My pillow was soaked with blood from the hole in my head. I had no idea of the damage done so I laid praying in shock.

My mother ran to get something to help stop the bleeding. She returned with a towel, applying pressure to my head. The blood flow soaked the towel in seconds and I could feel myself drifting into unconsciousness, and fight with all I had not to. Though feeling dizzy and semi-unconscious, I could hear my mother begging him to take me to the hospital.

I remember looking over at my brother and praying he would be okay. I desperately hoped my brother would not be his next victim. I was scared as hell, knowing the harm he could do to my little brother.

Thank God, he was stupid enough to allow us to leave the house. The plan was to run away. The excuse my momma used was we were only going to the drug store to get some bandages. I never understood what would make this man allow us to leave knowing how bad he beat us. But I was thankful he did.

My mother got us in the car and sped out of the apartment complex like a crazy woman. I laid in the back seat with my mind fixed on him chasing us. I imagined once he realized he let my mother go, taking us with her, he would realize his mistake coming after us and making us return to the house to finish us off.

Pulling up to our grandmother's house, my mother jumped out the car and ran in. I laid still in fear of him coming, not waiting him to catch me. I crawled out the door of the car. I had to get in the house as fast as possible. In my mind, he was pulling up any minute.

Once I was on the ground, I heard my grandfather's voice in my ear. I could not see clearly and was feeling my way with my hands when my grandfather picked me up from the sidewalk. He carried me into the house and put me on the couch in the den.

My aunt sat at the table next to me holding my hand and trying to assure me I would be okay.

Yeah right, was all I could think…*what about next time?* Yes at my young age, the events I had witnessed had now become a part of my reality. I knew my mother would go back *just like every woman I saw get beat did.*

I could hear the ambulance's siren as they came closer to the house. I felt a little relief knowing the police would be with them and we would be safe for the moment. After having my head bandaged and finally put in the ambulance, we headed to the hospital.

My mother explained to the police what happened, but I could hear guilt in her voice as if she was at fault for being beat. I just looked at the side of her face as she talked. *What is her problem?* This question weighed heavily on my mind. Here is her chance to put him in jail and it wasn't even remotely part of her conversation.

While in the hospital, I was left in the room alone. I experienced just how full of fear I was. I was going out of my mind looking under the bed and at the door. My fear was so great that I swore he was near and coming for me. I felt as if I was waiting for his face to appear and kidnap me.

After being treated, we returned to my grandmother's house. The phone calls between my mother and this man started immediately. It did not take any time before she put me back inside those walls. Just weeks before we had been covered in our own blood, damn near killed and she walked into the apartment as if nothing ever happened.

The blood had been washed off the walls. However, the memory of the scenes that took place between those walls had nowhere to go. Those events flashed as daily reminders in my mind. To make matters worse, my mother told us the court made her go back to him. I sat on the couch that day when she told me that, wondering if she really thought I would believe that bull.

Regardless of the reason or excuse, she took our asses back. No one could have made me go back and hope to live under the same roof with this man, no body.

But again what was I going to do?

Weeks went by and all my mother could do was lay in bed recovering from the internal injuries she suffered. My brother and I had to stay in the house while he was at work. We would entertain one another by playing games like leap frog to pass the time.

I wasn't sure of what my mother was feeling or going through mentally, but I did realize how foul she could be. She would tell him that she could not rest, because we were noisy all day and would not listen to her. In short, she was the reason we got our asses whipped most of the time.

Boy…boy, talk about love.

That is the kind of bull she did that made me start to hate being alive. I never believed nothing she had to say or did from then on.

To allow us to stay in this situation and get us in trouble with the man that beat the hell out of us was too much for me to swallow. To top it off, I found out that the day he beat us was the day they got married. Or the day she allowed him to adopt my brother, whichever day it was…that day should have been the last day he was a free man. She turned right around and allowed him to adopt me too. I was pissed. I could see no escape.

I had to carry his name. It was made official as I stood there in court being reminded that I would be exposed to his violence from that day thereafter.

Looking for comfort, I befriended an older woman who lived across the parking lot in the apartment complex. I do not recall how I started talking to this woman, but she gave me just what I needed when I needed a peace of mind and a way to cope with the hell I lived in.

She was older and in a wheelchair. She allowed me to talk about what was happening at home. She taught me how to cook *tomato soup and grilled cheese sandwiches were her specialty.* She gave me the strength to return to that apartment at night.

I held on for years to her words "your mother will do whatever it takes to provide for her children". *I knew she was giving me all she could and an excuse for my mother's actions.* No, I was no fool.

I knew she did not know how to help me! *But she did try.* Her words helped me many years later in my own motherhood. Years later her words would also help me to understand my own mother's choices.

Once my mother healed, she started working at a hospital at night. That meant we were at home alone with him. And this son of a mother sucker, with his sick mind made me bathe in front of him and he would even wash me at times. I was old enough to bathe myself. He was not concerned with washing me, but fondling me. Then he would make me get in the bed with him naked.

He would lay against me with his underwear off…

Not sure what he was getting out of it, I would lay there scared and praying. Thank God he never actually had sex with me.

Hold on, to make it crazier for me, I got bold and told my mother about what he was doing to me and she did not believe me! Or she just didn't do crap. *No it didn't end there….give me a moment to collect myself. I still suffer mentally when I relive this part of my life. And the scar on my head will never let me forget it.*

Seeing No Way Out

L et me tell you how this man showed his love. I call it, *the peacemaker*! He would give a gift to soothe an ass kicking. However, as sure as I am writing my story there were many other beatings.

He was notorious for buying her love and she bought into it. Arlington High School would become a landmark in my life. This house was located in the neighborhood behind the school. If those walls could talk, they would tell horror stories about our time spent there.

Since they cannot, let me...

The house on Daniel Drive! This street went in a big ass circle, with a never-ending sidewalk that knew my 'worried' walk with every circle I made. Their home was a big, empty, four-bedroom, three-level house. *I refuse to lay claim to that house.* The fights in this house happened on a regular basis. I even caught slaps in the face several times.

I received those slaps after doing something he did not see fit, like tasting the Kool-Aid with the same spoon I stirred it with. Or getting caught staring into space and failing to acknowledge him when he spoke to me.

My brother had to endure the touch of this man. There was a time that he hemmed my brother in the garage. Before it was over, he beat him with a belt in the bathroom. He beat him so bad that my brother messed on himself.

My mother spent very little time outside the house, because when she was out she was accused of screwing around. There was this time when she was in school learning how to prepare taxes. In his mind, she was meeting someone. Get this. He was taking her and picking her up, so how bold could she be? *Is that crazy or what?*

The fighting got worse each time. One night, my mother woke up only to find him standing over her with a skillet in hand. Somehow she made it out of the house. Even though I was awakened by the arguing, I played sleep. He came into my room to wake me up and made me sit with him on the stairs. He explained to me how much he loved us and how my mother made him do bad things.

His attempts to try and make me feel like I had to except his apologies didn't work. I just did not want to do anything to make him mad.

My mother ran across the street to a neighbor's house. She called and talked him into leaving for the night. He returned the next day, acting like nothing happened. My mother welcomed him with open arms.

I was tired and wanted out of this mess. I began to talk to a girl in school and she turned me on to suicide. I wasn't sure if she knew what she was talking about. However, I started wanting to die even more. I started trying to choke myself until I felt like throwing up. I even put my face in my pillow to try suffocating myself. I tried putting a trash bag over my face, but this method created too much fear.

I even attempted to drown myself.

I damn near choked to death, but this method just wasn't working for me. I could not figure out how to make this pain go away and none of my attempts helped.

We played with two boys that lived across the street. One day the mother overheard me talking to her oldest son. He was questioning me about the fights at home. I told him about my thoughts of dying, and those were the words his mother overheard.

His mother did not address my comment until the night we came home and momma's husband had broken into the house. After he kicked her ass, he would leave. Momma would try to find ways to secure the house. We hoped this would keep him from entering while we slept or was not there.

When we had to leave the house, we would open all the curtains and turn on all the lights. This would allow us to see into the house when we pulled in the driveway at night. But he would find a way in when he wanted. Hell I knew nothing we did could actually keep him out.

This particular night, we pulled up and he was standing in the kitchen. Seeing the headlights of the car, he hauled ass out the back door. He was no fool. He knew momma would call the police if she had the chance.

Times like that told me he wasn't as crazy or shell shocked as everyone tried to make me believe he was. Momma backed the car into the neighbor's driveway across the street. She ran to their door to have them call the police. The police rode through the neighborhood and checked the house for him.

Sitting on the trunk of the car in our neighbor's driveway, our friend's mother came out to comfort us, my brother and me. She used this time to talk to me about the conversation she overheard between her son and I from a few days earlier Hearing the fear I was holding on to and how I felt about him hurting us, she passed a sense of faith to me.

She talked to me about the Lord and how He watches over us. She told me the star above our house that night was an angel of protection. That angel was there just to watch over me. I held on to the story she told me and I did my best to believe in what she said. I needed some reassurance that we would live through the night.

He soon returned home at momma's request and the fighting continued. I just did my best to stay out of his way. I really started to care less about what he did to my mother. Hell, even she didn't give a damn. She allowed him to repeat the beatings.

I found myself isolated.

I started spending the night at my friend's house as much as possible. I took long walks in the neighborhood to stay away. I would make up games in my head to play when I could not get away. I even found myself beating the hell out of my male dolls. I secretly wished I would be taken from my mother…out of that house and away from that life.

Just as I knew it would, the fights escalated and our eyes eventually held a story that would leave us traumatized.

Coming in from school one afternoon, I had a funny feeling in my stomach. As my brother and I approached the door, I felt like I needed to turn around and run. I opened the door to let us in, instantly, I knew something was wrong. He called out my name and told me to "come here". My brother stepped inside the door. My mother was in a robe standing at the top of the stairs leading to the basement.

He held a shotgun in his hand…next to her head. Without a doubt, the fights were headed to a close, in my head. There had never been a gun involved and this was the same gun given to my mother for protection by grandfather.

I was sure that added fuel to his fire to see a gun was in the house and it was there to kill him. The scene before my eyes I knew played a big part of the funny feeling in my stomach when I arrived home. I had this feeling several times before.

That little voice inside warned me. I couldn't find the strength to act on these feelings or warning.

He pulled my mother down the stairs to the basement and made us follow. We sat through hours of watching our mother being beat naked. He hit her with the gun, phone, and banged her around from wall to wall. I was ready to die or at least I thought that would be the consequence we had to face for our mother's decision to let him back in her life.

I was building up the nerve to run and if I was caught so be it, we were dead anyway. With a gun involved, I knew for sure momma was going to be killed. I wondered what would happen to us. Or would we be killed too?

I asked if I could go to the restroom. When I reached the hall leading to the restroom, feeling uneasy, I looked around. He had positioned himself in such a way, he could watch me. He told me not to shut the door.

There went my chance! See, I knew he wasn't crazy!

Me making it up the stairs and out the door, I just did not see it happening. We spent several more hours in the basement of this house. We were hoping and praying, and watching him beat the life out of our mother.

Somehow, she calmed him down. She was able to talk him into getting out of the house. She had him take us all to the store. How the hell she managed this I still don't know, but I was so relieved. So she used our hunger as the excuse to leave the house. Food was the furthest from my mind but if it got us in the public, I claimed I was starving.

Once in the store, momma found the courage to tell him we weren't leaving with him. He became hot. With so many people around, the only thing he could do was turn around and walk away.

I pleaded with my mother to call the police. But she assured me she had it under control. We walked around the front of the store, looking through the window to see if he was still outside. When she felt the coast was clear we walked out. I was not feeling her method of escape at all. As we walked out the store, we had to break for the Baskin Robbins.

He was on our ass.

We hit the door of the Baskin Robbins screaming, shaking and showing fear for our lives. The man inside jumped over the counter in shock himself, I'm sure he was thinking, *what the hell?*

He locked us inside the store just in time! The stranger's quick reaction saved us and stopped him from getting his hands on us again.

Momma hollered, "He's going to kill us please call the police", as he stood at the door demanding her to bring her ass out. I was thinking, *why didn't she do this at the grocery store?* Hell, there were plenty of people in the store. Now we were locked in a store with only one other person. I was losing it in my mind at this point, and tired of this life. Inside, I felt empty. I didn't give a damn about anything. My mind was full of thoughts like, *Kill me and let it end, please!"*

Once again we were saved, but only for the moment. She would return for more… And several far worse ass beatings did occur. I'm sure you're thinking how much worse could it have gotten? Believe me when I say, it got worse!

I got so tired of momma trying to make me believe the stories…the stories of why she couldn't get away, stand up to this man and leave. I was tired of trying to stand up for her. I felt I could talk to some of his family members about our situation. They were the only people we were around now.

I believed they did not like what he was doing to us. But in the end, momma had the last word. Hell, I was a kid and she was willing to stay in her marriage. This made me start feeling hatred toward her.

Not strong enough to leave, my mother chose a way to escape this hell. I was the one who saved her life the morning she overdosed on her medication, on purpose. She was willing to die instead of saving us. *Isn't that some bull?* Watching my mother try to take her life opened my eyes. I could finally see how weak she was for this man, and how far she would go for him instead of us.

I had to walk her around in circles. I continued to try to keep her awake by putting a cold towel on her forehead, and talking to her non-stop. I cried in fear of the possible outcome. The phone rang. It was one of my aunts. She rushed over and my mother was taken to the hospital to have her stomach pumped. She lived to see yet another ass kicking, and we continued to suffer with her for the next couple of years.

Whenever she found the strength to leave, she also found her way back to him. Or he would find ways to torment the person's house we stayed in. This happened so much that we finally resorted to living from motel to motel. He attempted to kidnap us right off the streets! He promised to never hit us again. He'd say anything to get her to get in the car.

I could walk you through so many days of not knowing if we would live to see tomorrow. But the thoughts become too painful, just as if I was living in the moment of one of these horror scenes.

I can tell you that at this point in my life, I felt unloved. I was put in one bad situation after another because of her decisions and now with her abuser. I knew these things, but I did not realize how these events would negatively affect me in the years ahead.

To this day, having been a mother for twenty years, I will never understand how my mother was so screwed up in the head….putting us in such danger. Through this abusive period, she jeopardized her own life, many others, and especially the lives of her kids. Russian roulette is the name of that dangerous game and let me tell you, she played it to the fullest.

My Glimpse of Hope

I n 1980, I thought I would finally felt free of the physical and mental abuse; *however, I still experienced it in my dreams.* My stepfather, *the man who spent time in jail and was named on my birth certificate,* came back into my life.

Spending time with him and his wife was like being in heaven, compared to the hell I had survived. There was no fighting and even when I knew they were mad, they argued behind closed doors. We spent time together and I learned how much this man really loved him some Tonie.

With all the suffering that I had endured, being loved was what I needed. But again, momma would not let that happen. She made sure our time together was cut short. She made up excuses why I couldn't be with my stepfather. I knew she feared I would tell him about the events we had seen because of her, and what her man had done to me.

She made me promise not to talk to him about it. And I did not. I wanted my stepfather in my life. I asked to live with him. After that, I did not see him anymore. My mother made sure I didn't leave her side.

My mother moved us into an apartment on the eastside, Post Road. This was her stomping ground. Life started to look up for us, until my mother felt it was time for her to date again. Yep, the men and partying was on. My brother's father started moving back into the picture. Then there were the men from her past who served as financial support. Sometimes they only appeared when she needed money. I felt she should have been helping us heal, but she was only making up for time missed in her own life. So she carried on as if the traumatic events we suffered were only a figment of the imagination.

Me, I hung out getting high, using this to deal with the pictures embedded in my mind. The nightmares became a nightly fight for me, and I started walking in my sleep. I outwardly dealt with my feelings through displays of anger. School became a joke. I did not want to be with my mother or in school. I did very little when I was in those environments. My mother was gone most of the time. If she wasn't at work, she was hanging with her new friends *a man that eventually became my uncle*).

My brother and I entertained each other on nights home alone.

Before long, my mother's ex found out where we were. *I felt my mother led him to us.* To escape, I really started running right into the drama the streets held for a young scared little girl. I spent time around the neighborhood, or at someone else's house. I only came home when I had to.

I hung with the babysitter from prior years, or anyone that could take my mind off my mother and her problems. My brother lost himself in T.V.

I must have been in the fourth grade, acting grown as hell. I hung with the older kids in the 'hood. I rode out every weekend to hang on the crowded street known as 38th. I began to sip on beer, or whatever the crew had in a cup…flirting with boys much older than me. I was just hanging' out there and I had it bad! I was young, dumb and hanging' with the wrong crowd.

I never stopped to think about how these new behaviors I was developing would affect my growth and to be real I didn't care.

I wasn't being beat. So even in the midst of these crazy events, I didn't feel the fear I was used to.

It didn't take long for me to pick up my mother's bad habits. While I was running away to comfort myself, in a sense, I was running right into a world that was yet to be revealed. Now, Tonie, herself had to deal with experiencing what the streets had in store and make decisions for her next move. I knew the ways that I used to entertain myself with wasn't healthy. I just didn't give a damn so life was becoming more and uglier for me.

Let me keep you ahead of the game. I didn't like the pain inflicted on me but I used pain to soothe the pain. I know it did not make any sense. However, nothing made sense to me at this time. So I rolled with the events the streets presented to me. I would say for the most part, I became a pro with dealing.

I was friends with a white girl, who stayed a couple of doors down in the same apartment building. One afternoon we got to talking about our sexual experiences. She told me how her father would come home early to have sex with her. *??? I thought!* There were men in my mother's life that by now had put me in some awkward situations. But not my father! I really did not believe her, so she dared me to watch. This would be her way of proving to me that she was screwing her father. To me she didn't see anything wrong with what she was going through. I mean she boasted about this it as if it was an affair.

The next day I learned she was telling the truth. I could not believe it even after seeing it with my own two eyes. We stood outside dancing to the song, *Double Dutch Bus*, laughing and acting silly. She kept her mind on the time and was determined to prove she was telling the truth.

When it got close to the time her father would be home, we went upstairs to her apartment to find me a spot to hide. I hid in her parent's bedroom closet. This gave me the perfect view to see what I was so curious to see.

Her father showed up and it was on. My nerves were going crazy, as my heartbeat raced with every step he took while making his way up the stairs. I was so scared I'd be caught in their house. To my surprise, his mind was on taking care of business before anyone else made it home.

It all happened just as she described to me the day before.

I watched through the crack in the door as this man kissed and rubbed on his daughter as if she was his woman…she was very much into it too. *This is crazy* is all I could think. I witnessed them climb into bed after taking off their clothes and having sex like adults. This man was having sex with his own child.

The thought overwhelmed me causing flashbacks of my fearful and close run-ins with men. I bolted out of the closet like a bat out of hell. Startling him, he hollered as I hit the stairs not looking back. When I made it home, I told my mother the story of how I ended up in the closet and seeing this scene.

I wanted her to call the police.

My friend showed up at my door and begged me not to tell, but it was too late. I had to tell the story one more time. I told the woman that came with the police to investigate. I do know that her mother showed up shortly afterwards. I was not sure if they would help the girl, because she assured me her mother knew what was going on.

She said her mother never did anything to stop or confront the activities of her father. In that same week, the family disappeared (moved out).

To this day, I'm not exactly sure what happened to my friend. I just wanted to help. This experience stuck with me. I refused, from that point on; to never let another one of my mother's male companions put me in any sexual situations.

Right before our stay in Indianapolis ended; my mother met the man who would save me. He provided us with a way out. A way out of the hell my mother couldn't seem to get out of her path. He spent a lot of time at our house from jump. He had a woman living in an apartment complex not too far from ours. And of course, there was some drama involved.

The difference was, it was not in our house. I learned about this drama by listening to adult conversations.

I remember him showing up one night with his hand bandaged. He told us the war stories of how he and his girl got into a fight because he did not come home. My mother took this as a cue to make her move on him. In a blink of an eye, he was living in our house fulltime. During the next closed door conversation, I eavesdropped. I learned he was moving us out of State.

I grew close to him. For the first time, I had a man in my life that showed sincere love for me, understood my fears and cared about what I had been through. This isn't to say some of the other men didn't care, but up until this point momma had made me keep quiet. So now that my mouth was free to talk, I talked about the hell my family was freshly out of and I was scared it was not over. And it was not! I pleaded for us to get out of the situation in Indy.

I often brought up the topic of us needing to leave.

The morning came when my mother was chased to the door with our abuser on her heels. I heard the pounding on the door and the fear in her screams. I looked out the window and saw him getting out of the car. I ran down the stairs to let her in the house. I unlocked the door. While running to get to the phone, and a wasp stung me on my back. But you can best believe that nothing, not even a wasp sting, stopped me from making that 911 call.

Later that afternoon, my mother's boyfriend showed up. While my mother was away from home, he stayed there to keep me calm. I was ironing some clothes and heard a noise. With my heart pounding, I went to the back window to see what the noise was. I looked down to see my mother's ex was back and trying to get into the house.

I ran up the stairs into the room to wake up my mother's boyfriend. I jumped on the bed, causing the iron to fall on my thigh. I didn't care.

All I cared about was making sure this man didn't get in the house and beat me again. My mother's boyfriend went downstairs to confront my mother's ex. But her ex ran off. *Just as he did, when any man got in his face! Punk ass nigga…*I was taken to the hospital for a second-degree burn.

Experiencing my deepest fear first hand, my mother's boyfriend decided it was time to relocate me in order to keep me safe. I agreed! He left to find us a new home. He checked out California and Texas. He returned and announced his decision. Houston would be our next home. My mother left ahead of us by plane. With a truck backed up to the back door, we gathered our belongings, packed the truck, and hit the road. Finally, we were headed toward the horizon of a new beginning and a new Tonie.

I hate to end here, but this part of my life affected me tremendously. It still frustrates with me to this today. I have worked to deal with the mental and physical wounds I suffered. I use different methods that work for me and keep me going.

Writing is one of those methods I use to deal with the wounds. Writing is therapeutic for me. And I also hope by putting my story in print, it will give others hope that things can get better. However, I soon realized I prefer to talk about most of those situations. This way, those bad memories that affected me deeply will not all be in black and white to read for the rest of my life.

Even with the story that is left untold, the crack in the cement has been opened and some of the spout of my past is now before your eyes.

Through my writing, I believe I've provided the vision needed in order to understand the seeds embedded in my head. I pray the picture I've painted for you through my writing is crystal clear.

Can you see what I saw?

Embedded Seeds helped me look at my past for what it was and how it affected me. The whys and how's! *Embedded Seeds* describes some of the events in my life starting from the tender age of three. These memories in my head have weighed heavily on my heart for years and these memories did play many roles in my decision making as I grow older.

So...so...so...

Be prepared to see those decisions I made from these experiences I have now shared...you will find my next path in, Love for the Streets, as I walk you through how these Embedded Seeds affected and manifest in who I became.

Personal Writings

The Best of Both Worlds or Not

In 1971, I was born to a white mother and a black father in Indianapolis, Indiana. Not everyone accepted interracial couples back then.

I didn't have a problem having a lighter complexion than the black side of the family or darker than the white side of my family.

Once I began to notice the treatment of people based on their skin color, I started to understand the way I was treated.

Being around either side of my family caused conflict. Most of the conflict arose from the fact that my mother had biracial children. My brother and I were aware of the difference people made between us and other children.

The black side of my family had minor problems with us. Most of the time, every child was loved equally. Our apparent mixed racial heritage was a problem on the white side, affecting how they loved and treated us. We were unacceptable and felt like this for years to come.

The white side of my family displayed unnatural affection and behavior when we were around them. The obvious differences between the two sides of my family caused me to ask questions.

At that time a very good friend of the family, my "play" sister, explained racism to me. I was strong-willed at a young age. I didn't allow the way I was being treated affect my thoughts or feelings. I've always felt I was unique by having the best of both worlds.

Experiencing racism made me fight even more to resist any negative effects. This pissed off the ones that saw their negative attitudes bounce and roll off me like rain falling on the hood of a freshly waxed car.

In public, people we encountered like teachers, kids, and even strangers only made positive remarks to my brother and me. In school, I did experience problems with females. I pretty much summed this up as jealousy. Once they looked past my outer appearance and began to know me from the inside out, we formed friendships.

Very seldom did I encounter racial remarks in school or in our neighborhoods. When I did, I had enough strength to overlook them. I believe being around both sides of my mixed racial heritage at a young age helped me understand that I was not alone. I saw interracial couples and biracial children. I also had to be there for my younger brother.

We usually only experienced being treated different when were around our white side of the family.

My white grandmother held on to stereotypes she learned from her upbringing. It was clear that she only accepted us to ensure she would be able to have her daughter in her life. As kids, my brother and I had to stay at our grandmother's house while our mother worked.

I can remember our grandmother allowing us to come inside the house to the room besides the back den only. When it was close to time for my mother to return from work, she would let us sit in the front room with the door open.

We never received Christmas presents from our grandmother. I really didn't want one from her because I felt that accepting something from her would be accepting her.

At that time I didn't accept her. I used to make jokes about any and everything I discovered different about the black and white sides of our families. My brother would question me about why our grandmother treated our cousins one way and us another. I'd just tell him those jokes to make him laugh. For me, they were a joke and not worth my tears.

Then there was my mother's oldest sister. She was a carbon copy of our grandmother. She tried to inflict the same type of mistreatment our grandmother used. She would invite us over for dinner. We had to eat outside, only coming in the house to use the restroom. She used stupid reasons why we had to stay outside from the time we arrived to the time we left.

As we watched her son and our cousins run in and out of the house, I remember telling my brother they were stupid and we were too good to be in her dirty house anyway.

When we were much older, we realized our mother was aware of how her side of the family treated us. She started talking openly about her family's attitudes towards us. She tried to justify their ignorance.

What a slap in the face. My life experiences and becoming a mother of five beautiful children has given me the courage to speak my mind. I have noticed a change in my family because I have been vocal about my feelings.

To this day, the white side of our family is still so backwards in how they view race…among other things as well. I've learned that I can't change them. As long as I receive respect as a human being, and my children are not mistreated, I can deal with their ignorance. I pray for the day the entire human race see each other as humans and not colors.

Admiring My Kids

Let's talk about the ones I strongly admire. Yes, my kids. I could write a book on their lives. My kids are the five craziest beings on earth. Not one of them has the same personality.

They have unique minds. With looks so amazing, similar to one another, and still there are five different demeanors dancing daily in my home.

Each with a unique touch of self-beauty that spreads thickly over each and every one they meet.

I have four boys and there is a wide variety of activities displayed daily. Such as their likes, wants and plans to reach future goals. I watch them develop their strong minds and firm cut bodies. I admire the beauty in how handsome they have become in every growth span. They practice strange ways to show their love. They are becoming more ambitious as they mature.

I notice them imitating one another, showing that cute unique quality of displaying affection and love. I sometime admire them from afar, watching all the siblings. If I made my presence known, their shy and introverted characteristics would appear. These last couple of years, my sons, had developed a new competition among one another.

These competitions show how they have developed the art of dressing flashy, sporting funky braids, and working extremely hard toward excelling in the sports of their respective choice. Not to mention, I have one son who thinks he is the finest of the four. Let it be known, I have four of the most special, brightest, blessed, and divinely chosen sons that any mother could want.

Last but not least, my daughter. She is the treasure in my soul. She has shed light on darkness, when I thought I was at the end of my rope. She brings comfort to my days. She is truly an angel in my life and shines like a beautiful diamond in my heart. It seems she was brought into my life to protect and guide me at times.

She reminds me that there is more to living than the life I lived. She shows maturity, strength, happiness and love in everything she gives. She is truly one of a kind.

My Commitment

What is P.E.E.P.S?

People Encouraging Empowerment Perceiving Success

For the moment, allow me to put a question in your mind and before you answer, give it at least three minutes to marinate. *What is wrong with the youth of today?*

Now what came to your mind first?

Our youth, is who the P.E.E.P.S are gearing up for. We must all not only answer this question but do something about it.

I, Tonie Punch will reach out however many times it takes to bring a lost youth back, I will buy, borrow, or beg for another set of arms to reach out with.

By all means necessary!

Why?

Because I too was…*XYZ!*

I was born right here in Indy, 1970's, to the world of both black and white, so life was ugly for me from day one… now add drama. Webster hasn't provided me with a word to this day to describe the emptiness, hurt and anger I held in the depth of my heart for the hell I heard, seen and eventually had to endure physically in the city we call Nap-town.

The names designed for bi-racial children started the mental abuse; however it grew to the fist that weighted a ton as it connected with my jaw or head, now it was physical. The ass kicking's for me was not with a belt but a fist, a wall or the door breaking the fall as I landed. Watching how others use drugs to ease the pain, gave me what I needed to see through the shame.

Life here for me was hell or at least that's what I thought until I was relocated to Texas. Oh boy, it was on then. With the lil street I thought I had mixed with a big city, it wasn't a pretty picture at all.

For several years, *SEVERAL* to come my life was like a building collapsing as the wrecking ball (family, friends, peers, streets, abuse, drug, sex,) slowly but surely left that life I claim in a pile of broken rocks.

Don't get me wrong I went down fighting (using every drug I put my hands on) just to say I could hang.

Reality, I was self-destructing.

What was I to do?

Remember the saying "young and dumb?"

Yep>>> Tonie!

Confused, depressed and scared as hell, refusing to believe that I even needed help.

To be honest I was so far gone to the streets that help was the last thing on my mind. Hold on now, we are talking destruction from start (between five and six) and still working on the closure. When you come through the life experiences I've survived, you learn to take life as it comes.

Loneliness

How many of us truly know this emptiness? What about our youth? Now add destruction of loneliness in to the life of a troubled youth. Damn, that's not pretty!

Have you, as a family member, friend, or maybe just a concerned individual, hypothetically thought to ask the question, how are you feeling?

At home, in school, even around family members and friends, I felt lonely. Understanding compassion or just comfort is what I was seeking; from someone, anyone!

The level of maturity I developed was higher than my reach, *they all said*!

Nevertheless, reality was in my face and the only advice I received (from family, friends, teachers, and adults) was stay in a child's place. Grown up issues was the name of the game and for so many reasons I had to play.

I was in the middle of the grown-ups issues (lying, abusive arguing, fighting, and drugs) all that happened and all that would come, I too dealt with.

Who
Who
Who was I to turn to?
The streets!!!

They had an answer, one that worked for me… the streets posed the same people—people just like me. The best of it all, there were no grown-up *only* issues.

Age played no part. We all shared (hurt, confusion, pain, and anguish) true loneliness. The streets provided us the comfort and understanding.

The streets became a way to fight the feeling of loneliness (drinking, drugs, sex, and crime) for me and many like me in order to survive the hurt and pain.

Now tell me who cares?

Why do our youth go to the streets? Because we as adults don't give them the answers they seek or a way to deal with their feelings. If we continue to treat our youth in these unhealthy ways, we will open the door for the streets to teach them the only way it knows!

I know how you are…

These can be words of destruction.

We notice all the flaws but never the changes.

WHY???

I know you, how you are, what you're capable of, and how you do what you do…All these statements set my blood to boiling and destruction to molding.

These words have formed over the years like a double edge sword piercing my ears (from my family, to my friends, even in my relationships); the voices behind those words fuel a flame of anger from deep inside of me.

All the negative shows and none of the positive make a difference. Reality, No! You don't know me. You only think you do. You know what you choose to see in me. You know what your eyes are open to.

If you knew me, the true me, everything you would see would make you understand me, love me, and except me for who I truly am.

Assumptions are all you hold. Assuming you know why my situation happened or why things are how they are.

Open minds, what ever happened to having one? Listening without being judgmental and accepting that nothing and definitely no one is perfect. Trauma can and does happen.

Sit back and answer, how do these words make you feel and how angry can you become listening to them? So why do we allow the cycle of these statements to stay in our life and pass them on to our children.

Our parents swore they know every hair on our body an every movement we made and we as parents feel the same.

No, we don't know our children truly, like we think. Just as we changed and matured, they do to. In these days, our youth are growing up even quicker. So stop the "I know how you are" and ask how are you now!

Choose a Path and Follow It

D o I choose the easy path? Or do I choose the right path? Making decisions where difficult back in the day and are hard as an adult.

So why don't we as adults keep it real with our youth and give them the understanding of making chooses and the challenges that comes with them? Growing up in a destructive home and looking for understanding and love that was not being found; therefore made making positive chooses for my next step(s) impossible.

Spending years looking and listening to all the games and cons everyone around me where playing to get by only showed me the tick of my future trade(s)!

On that note I asked on of the teens I talk to, what do you want to accomplish in your life? When you're moving forward (home, school, ect...) how do you choose a path? Do you understand that anything worth having, you must work for? Or do you just look for the easiest way to make your next step not putting any effort into it?

Elias is a fourteen year old, has a stable family life, don't know poverty and he still faced struggles. His respond to my questions was summed up into this answer:

I am at a point in life where I have to choose a path, so which path do I choose? The questions I now must ask myself are, the right way or the easy way! Sure I want to choice the right way but its feels better the easy way. I am honestly having trouble choosing the right path because I am essentially lazy and I prefer to take the easy way through life.

And the easy way usually tends to get me into trouble; therefore I have to find a way to cope.

Meaning, I have actually thought about using drugs to deal with my issue(s). Thank God, the conversations I've had with Tonie Punch replaying in my head made me cancelled that phone call and experiencing the risk of visiting "another world", as Tonie would say.

At this time in my life I see only two roads to choice from: being a slacker and druggie or rise up to a higher level by applying myself. I am use to performing with the bare minimum of effort that I usually take the easy path.

Tonie, I want you to know that I thank you for intervening in my life at this time that gives me confidence that I can work harder with your help to reach my dreams and make better choices for here on. Thank you and I am only one there are so many more that need you to.

His answer to me was clear and very understandable, because without being able to express his-self fully how can he make positive chooses!

Without effective and direct communication allowing him to talk straight up, I know he would have made a destructive decision that would have put him on an even rocker road. We cannot allow our youth to stay stuck in making easy chooses for their life.

Open a door for them to speak their inter feelings without being judgmental but understandable. Remember we all have a story!

We all had to make choices!

Momma My Ass!

To live without spirituality and happiness for me would be not to continue life. In the journey of mistakes and experiences at thirty-five, I have come to realize that I can overcome any obstacle in my life.

Having spirituality and happiness within my heart and soul gives my mind a stress-free way to deal with daily issues and comfort in making peace with what I can't change.

Regardless of what I go through in life, having spirituality and happiness is being at peace. To be at peace gives me a way to be patient in order to put in action the ability to let go and let GOD!

My motto is "Do what I can today and pray for knowledge to handle tomorrow; not to dwell on how a person may negatively react toward me, but to be my best toward people."

There was a time I would say what a beautiful mother I have, with long dark hair and sky blue eyes. My mother spoke with confidence, possessing an amicable personality.

She was a special person and able to befriend anyone. Once I got to know her heart, I saw a woman of great misery, confusion, filled with hatred, and so eccentric.

To see her (for me) is to see an evil spirit in the flesh. Darkness and unhappiness travels with her every step. This woman hurts everyone close to her. Her definition of love is the opposite of the true meaning.

To seek and destroy is the only love she inflicts. Animals have been the only form of companionship to survive in and around her being. It's been that way for many years. To truly know her is to know Satan himself.

What a way to feel, huh?

I'm keeping it raw and real! Dealing with the issues of our youth today has shown me that mothers can be a root of destruction in their children's lives. To be a mother today, I truly can say I don't have to be how my mother was. I love the woman I have become. The road to healing has it wealth and today **the woman I am knows her purpose.**

I accept the will for my life and grow daily more spirituality and happier as my life develops. I am a mother of five and proud of who I am as a mother...to all the youth with momma drama, keep your heads up and break the cycle.

Regardless of who or where you come from change is possible once you realize it is your choice.

Not all mothers are worthy of carrying the name **"*mother*"**, but rest assure that one day they will face the choices they to humanly made.

Open your ears and minds to generational cycles; they are alive and just as we are suffering while seeking survival our mothers suffer seeking forgiveness.

Life still continues…

Me, Myself and Her

This cry inside of me has lived for many years. I have wanted answers to my questions. Why your own daughter? Now at 35, I still don't have answers.

I sometimes only feel deep confusion and hurt.

I'm a mother of five. I've been a mother for twenty years of my life now. I still can't understand how someone could intentionally inflict pain on a child.

Even with all the wrong choices I've made, I never tried to hurt my children in any way. I've traveled the wrong road too many times and allowed my actions to affect my family. But I never used being a mother as an excuse for my screwed up ways or how I chose to live. I accepted my wrongdoings, and did my best to learn from them and move on. It is my own fault I didn't always get back on the right track…right away.

Why would a mother cause problems over and over in a child's life? Situations that would cause hurt and pain to her child, distance and heartache for a lifetime? To internally feel the damage of her (**my mother**) lies told (just to hear herself talk) and physical abuse I suffered either directly or indirectly. I wonder did she truly understand the possible outcome. To hell with destroying her relationship with her child, but the destruction this hatred would cost her in her relationship with her grandchildren.

How can she wake up daily, go about her routine, sleep, or look in the mirror with a clear conscience? To top it off, she really believes she isn't doing anything wrong! Is this her way of coping?

My life hasn't been easy. It's a hard pill to swallow when those that did the most damage to me were family members. My reality was, they had a way of stomping you into the ground in a blink of an eye and would keep stomping if you let them.

Recollection of being a part of her (**my mother**) life, is to be used and controlled. Lying for her, covering up her mess, having to play the "momma" role for my younger brother, and having my head beat in for her mistakes was the only way to receive her grace.

As a young child, she made me lie about her whereabouts, who she was with, and where she was headed. In my desperate need for love, I did everything she asked of me and preformed exactly as I was instructed.

While she lived the street life, I was there for my brother and tried to be a kid at the same time. This became a major struggle in life for me. Being a "child" didn't last for long. Before I knew it, I was moving into my teen years and the streets were all I wanted.

Sometimes I was the only young girl hanging around adults who hung in the streets to partying hard. Just as I adapted to the lifestyle, fear and beatings walked through the door. I watched my mother get beat.

I then began getting beat for her. At the time, I thought maybe beating me would save her.

Hell, I didn't know.

I recall thinking, *which was worse? Watching or being included?*

Hoping it would make things better for my mother, I continued to cover up and lie for her. I believed the brightest star above our house was an angel sent by God to protect us and keep us alive. We constantly swayed between hospitals and motels.

We frequently changed schools like a pair of worn out running shoes. I wasn't afforded time to have a normal childhood and develop as a young girl should. I held close the need to escape my mother's issues which caused me to be confused and frightened.

I often felt the day would come when I would *have* to leave.

I didn't realize I would cause problems for my life and have some of the same issues I suffered through with her. This would be the seeds of destruction for me. No one ever hinted how this would carry over and affect my own children one day.

In order to get her way with the time and money of her male friends, different men were presented to me as my father and I was made to claim them as such. I know it was sick! In the back of my mind I tried to figure out how many more lies are there?

Why incorporate me into the lies? Every man my mother had been with and would get back with was my father! Let her tell it, the only choice I had was to go along with the mess. To this day I still wonder does she even know for sure who my father is or if she ever really cared.

Me, I felt I know who my father was and my father passed knowing his daughter and that's all that matters.

With all of her flaws she was blessed and saved. I thought time had come that we would finally start a different life and I could learn how to be a kid. I thought her new man was sent from heaven. He didn't give a damn about her past situations and took on her present ones.

Doing what he felt would give us a chance he moved us to Houston. This man was a father figure for my brother and me.

To this day he is still a part of my life and a grandfather to my children. Unfortunately, her (my mother) address was the only thing that changed when we moved to Houston. She was still evil as hell and even more at this point. It didn't take long to run away like everything else positive in her life.

I was tired! I had just about all I was going to take. I was in a new city, on new streets and with new friends. I was just so damn ready to get away from her. I quickly changed my personality, behavior and attitude.

I sought what I was missing at home in the likes of the streets and boys. I was no longer Tonie. I was Tee!

*Generational cycle...*I was now a part of the world I despised! I stayed on the run and went through whatever I had to in the streets, just so I didn't have to deal with her.

I skipped to several cities and States! I ducked, dodged, and hid from a woman I refused to have in my life anymore. The sadness about this is…as a result of my actions; I went through a living hell. I saw and survived unspeakable experiences. I truly felt that being in the streets was better than being at home.

I had…**Control**! She too became tired of my crap but she had a plan for handling me. She married my ass off at 14. Let her tell it, I wanted it more than she did. The marriage! To be honest, I did. But still that's no excuse to give away your fourteen year old daughter to a grown man without putting up a fight. To hell with me being pregnant!

She was a single mother most of my life so what was the difference? I feel this was her way to get me out of her life. This way she wouldn't have to worry about the police in her dysfunctional lifestyle because of my frequent running away from home. Matter of fact I know it was!!!

I disobeyed her and she had to find ways to make me suffer. And she did! She teamed up with my (at that time) husband in every unthinkable way to destroy my life. Her influences, along with those lips on her face are and have always been a chaos.

The stories go on and on. My relationship with my mother is still full of unbelievable actions designed to destroy my being and out of straight up hatred. I have not yet found understanding or away to let go of the need to know why. Why do you hate me so much? Why don't you allow me to screw up my own life?

Why have you always been the head and the tail of destructive events I, your daughter, had to survive? Do you know how much I do love you and want you to be a part of my life?

I know and God knows that has caused more harm than growth for me! That's sad....I know!

Me, Myself and Her...My Mother, and I still love her.

Who is Tonie Punch?

Today, this "new" day, I am a strong, positive, vocal, community activist and entrepreneur. But yesterday, I was in turmoil.

I have been homeless and hungry. I have indulged in drugs and alcohol, engaged in sexual impropriety and committed crime.

More importantly, I allowed myself to believe I had good reasons to place blame on other people, things and events.

The formative years of my life were for the most part, dark and full of misery. During this period, my hopes and dreams collided with a brutal reality. My emotions controlled my actions and sunshine was scarce. The hurt I experienced during this time was non-stop. By six years of age I knew about sex, physical and mental abuse, suicide, drugs and alcohol.

Throughout my childhood I experienced nightmarish rape and the worst part is that I knew my attackers. They were family and "supposed" family, neighbors and so-called friends. I was lost and often suicidal seeing very few alternatives to my situation. Witnessing and experiencing several tragic events in my life turned me into a walking time bomb.

My experiences in school and home gave me all the fuel I needed to search for love in all the wrong places. The streets gave me comfort but always left me in tragic situations. I ended up having no family, education or employment, but I did have five children and no idea what to do or where to begin. I stood in quicksand and was sinking fast because of the choices that led me to do whatever it took to eat, sleep and survive.

Turning Point

In my journey I met people and encountered moments that embedded (what I call) "seeds of faith" in me which sparked my desire for success and encouraged my mind towards freedom. Unfortunately, I didn't always process these "seeds" in a healthy way as I lacked insight and vision.

In the years that followed I used everyone who tried to help me or cared about me as I lived a life of crime and drugs. My lifestyle was self-destructive and hurtful even for my children.

In 1998, I spent time at Wackenhut Corrections in San Antonio, Texas, where I realized I had to use this time to improve myself. I wanted a better life for me and my children. I began to look for answers.

I developed a vision for a better Tonie after many lonely and empty nights. These visions aided me with dreams, goals and a plan!

1998, I returned to the outside world and with little support and no resources, I continued to make stupid mistakes. Feeling that the life I seen in jail would be hard to continue once, I was free. Back "on the bricks", a.k.a. the streets, I fell back into the trap of watching time pass and making no effort to change until I lost my best friend to a bullet.

I had a decision to make; give in to the system or leave Texas and the negative hold it had on me. I returned to Indianapolis even though I swore I never would.

Here were my earliest memories of life a nightmare that was still fully vibrant!

Despite this I held onto my new needs and beliefs that there was something more to life. Change was imminent. The old Tonie became a memory as the new Tonie emerged. I began to develop a new attitude of living one day at a time. Learning to love my failures because of the part they played in my forthcoming success.

My New Start Almost Ended Before It Began

Memorial Day, 2002, I allowed myself to be put in yet another predicament with the law. Now facing an eight year prison sentence, I had to fight. Standing on faith, opening up fully to my higher power and knowing I had changed, I was prepared for whatever was going to happen.

The Judge Berated Me AND My Husband in Open Court

July 2003, I experienced my higher power's will for my life, because even though the presiding judge berated me and my husband in open court saying I hadn't learned my lesson, God's grace prevailed and I never saw a single day of that 8-year prison sentence. Almost losing nearly a decade of your life and then all of a sudden being granted freedom makes you take a long hard look at the role you played in putting yourself in a situation where you gave someone else the power to determine how a large portion of your life plays out.

Stepping out on that very same faith that blessed me to continue to live, I learned humility. Despite numerous challenges, roadblocks, and empty promises from a myriad of public officials and private individuals of Indianapolis, who claimed to be philanthropists and supporters, I give of myself and past experiences to others.

Helping Others Reclaim Their Future by Sharing My Past

While I truly believe that book education is a good thing, I also know that there is no better teacher than experience. Because of this, my mission in life is to share my personal stories to help others understand how essential it is to make thoughtful decisions in your life. Nearly everything you go through in life is a direct result of the decision you make.

Once I understood that the misery I lived as an adult was largely influenced by decisions I was making (based on my childhood), nearly everything changed for the better. Not all at once, but it did begin to change once I changed.

Personal Message to Parents

There was a time (once I began living a different lifestyle) that I didn't think my children would be affected by the horrors of my past nor did I believe that it would hinder them as they grew.

The reality is that I was wrong.

Once their behaviors started really showing I realized how much my past affected their future.

So what I am saying in short **parents** is…understand you do play a major role in your child's outlook on life.

Please don't hear me say that you are the total reason for why your child or children are the way there are because **they too are responsible** for their decisions.

As a parent you may think that your child or children don't need to know what you're doing or why you do what you do, but more often than not they know what's going on especially if it is negative or hurtful.

We as parents can only hide so much from our children and I believe the major harm isn't done from what they see, but from having no one they feel they can talk to about what they've seen who will understand their thoughts on it.

A confused child won't turn to you. They turn to other children for answers (because they believe **you** either won't or aren't willing to understand and will only judge them) and as you know, other children don't have the right answers.

Are you as a parent faced with a child who feels misunderstood and you can see them headed down the wrong path? If so, have you thought about having a group discussion with an outside point of view?

Not only from a parent's perspective, but from the view of someone who was once a lonely, confused and mixed up child prone to negative behavior?

My journey has taught me how to recognize certain behaviors in parents and children (people in general) who feel like they have nowhere to turn and help them understand and deal with these emotions.

Some people my look at my past as a tragedy, but I see it as an opportunity to help others.

The only real tragedy would be if I learned nothing from all of the experiences of my youth, but that isn't the case.

I've learned a lot and have been helping others in similar situations find the will to survive and thrive in the face of whatever my come their way.

As long as you can breathe there is always hope.

Through my non-profit organization (Bring It To The Table) I facilitate creative ways of dealing with the past, understanding the here and now and moving towards a better tomorrow.

Please contact me if I can be of assistance in *your* life, the life of your child or the life of a child of someone you know who needs a little help to make it through and watch for the sequels to *"Don't Let The Pretty Face Fool Ya"*.

Be blessed,

Antoinette "Tonie" Punch

Call **1-888-289-1088**
Email: **info@toniepunch.com**
Or Visit: **http://www.ToniePunch.com**

Get updates on future books in this series straight to your cell phone! All you have to do is send a simple text message.

Text the word **tpunch** to: **713-678-0338**

When future books in this series are released, you will get a text message letting you know when and where to go and get your copy. **You will also get excerpts from other books in the series before *anyone* else sees them**.

Made in the USA
Coppell, TX
15 October 2023